Savannah and Its Surroundings

With Maps and Illustrations.

Marula

An imprint of Arcadia Publishing

Savannah and Its Surroundings
G.A. Gregory

A Marula Historical Reprint
Originally published in 1890

Published by Arcadia Publishing
Charleston SC

ISBN 978-0-7385-9482-8

Printed in the United States of America

For all general information contact Arcadia Publishing at:
Telephone 843-853-2070
Fax 843-853-0044
E-mail sales@arcadiapublishing.com
For customer service and orders:
Toll-Free 1-888-313-2665

Visit us on the Internet at www.arcadiapublishing.com

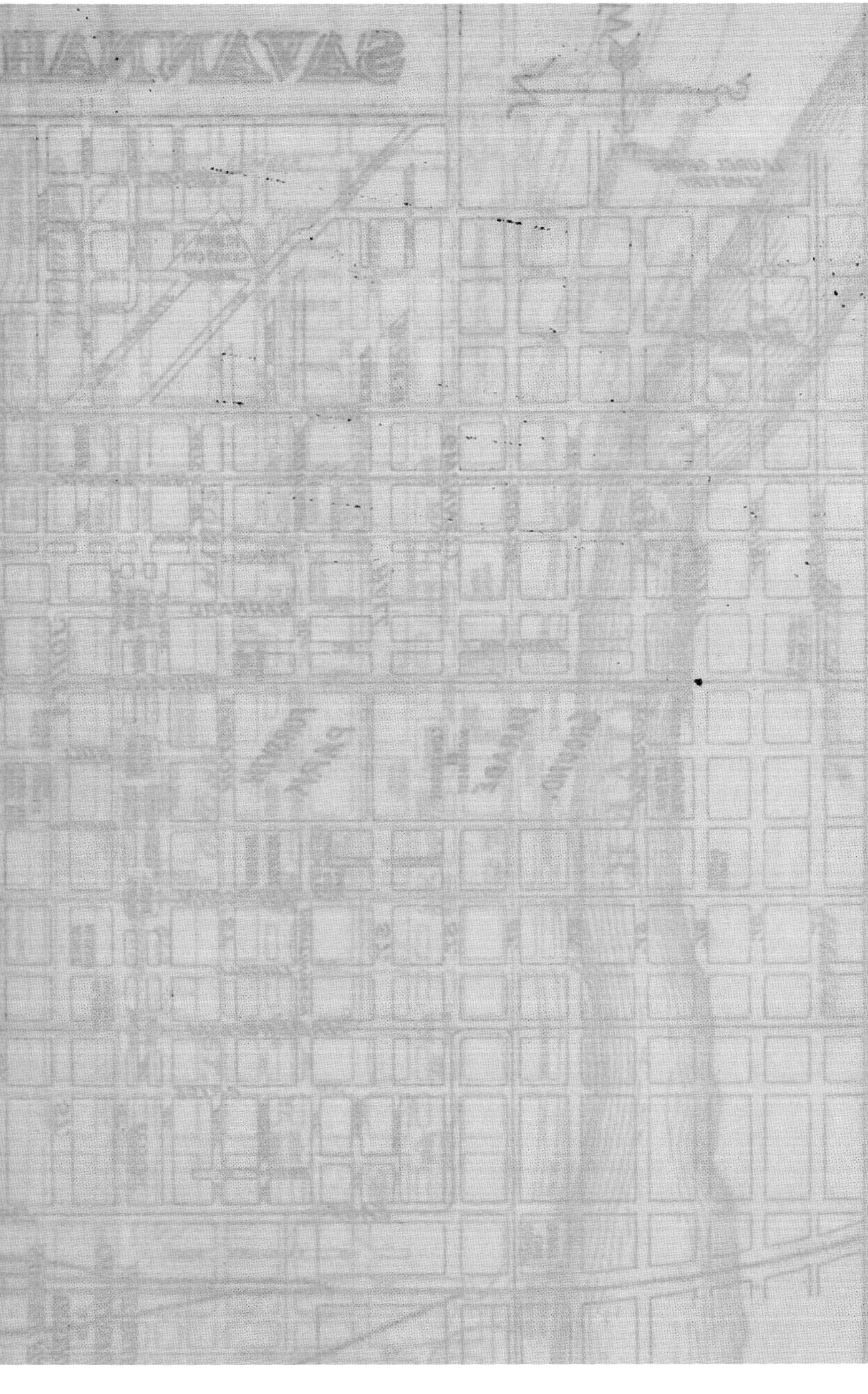

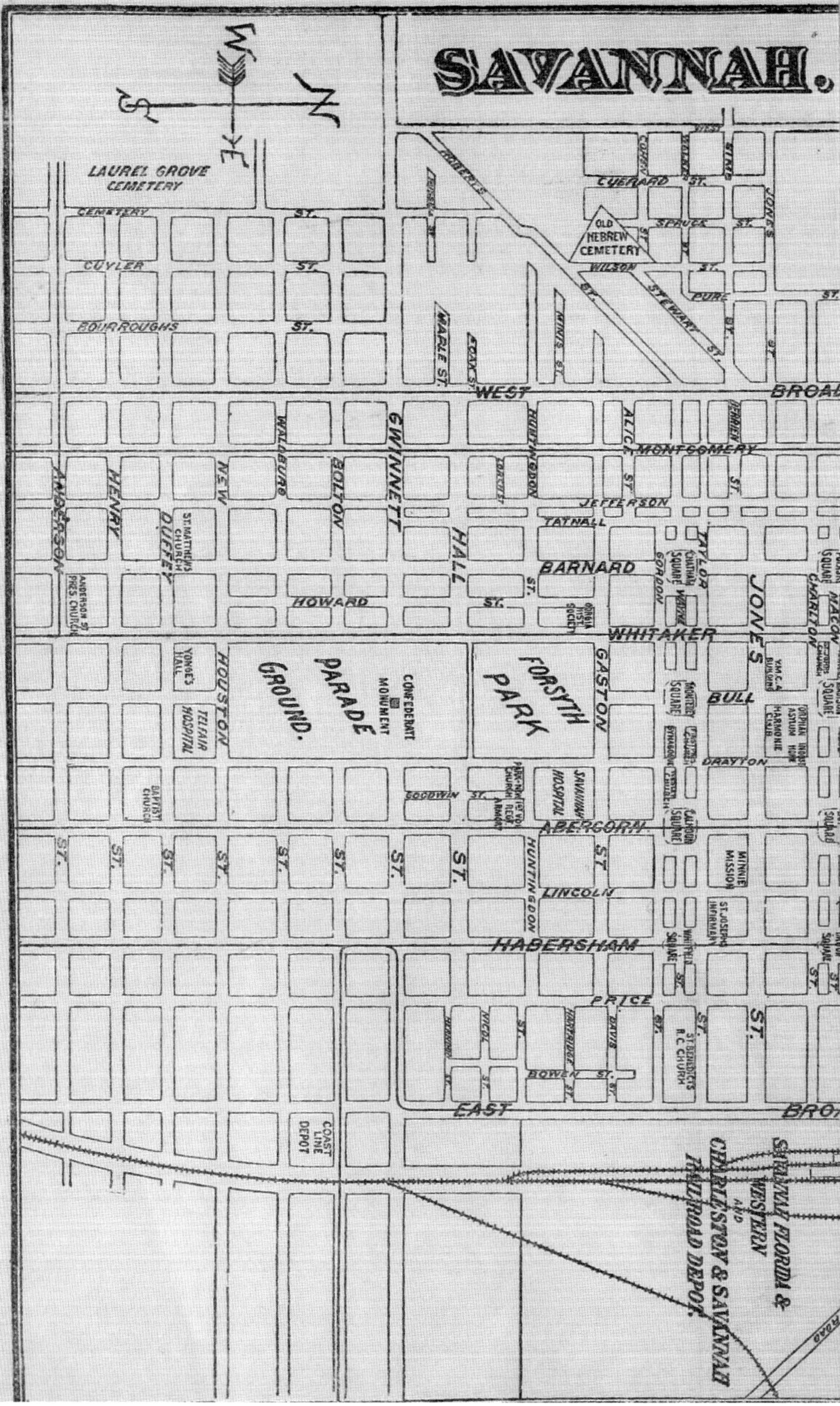
SAVANNAH.
LAUREL GROVE CEMETERY
OLD HEBREW CEMETERY
CEMETERY ST.
CUYLER ST.
BOURROUGHS ST.
WEST BROAD
MONTGOMERY ST.
JEFFERSON
TATNALL
BARNARD ST.
HOWARD ST.
WHITAKER
GASTON
BULL
DRAYTON
ABERCORN
LINCOLN
HABERSHAM
PRICE ST.
BOWEN ST.
EAST BROAD
JONES
GWINNETT
HALL
HOUSTON
HENRY
ANDERSON
DUFFEY
NEW
BOLTON
HUNTINGDON
FORSYTH PARK
PARADE GROUND.
CONFEDERATE MONUMENT
ST. MATTHEWS CHURCH
ANDERSON ST. PRES. CHURCH
YONGE'S HALL
TELFAIR HOSPITAL
BAPTIST CHURCH
SAVANNAH HOSPITAL
MINNIE MISSION
ST. JOSEPH'S INFIRMARY
ST. BENEDICT'S R.C. CHURCH
Y.M.C.A. BUILDING
HARMONIE CLUB
COAST LINE DEPOT
SAVANNAH FLORIDA & WESTERN AND CHARLESTON & SAVANNAH RAILROAD DEPOT.

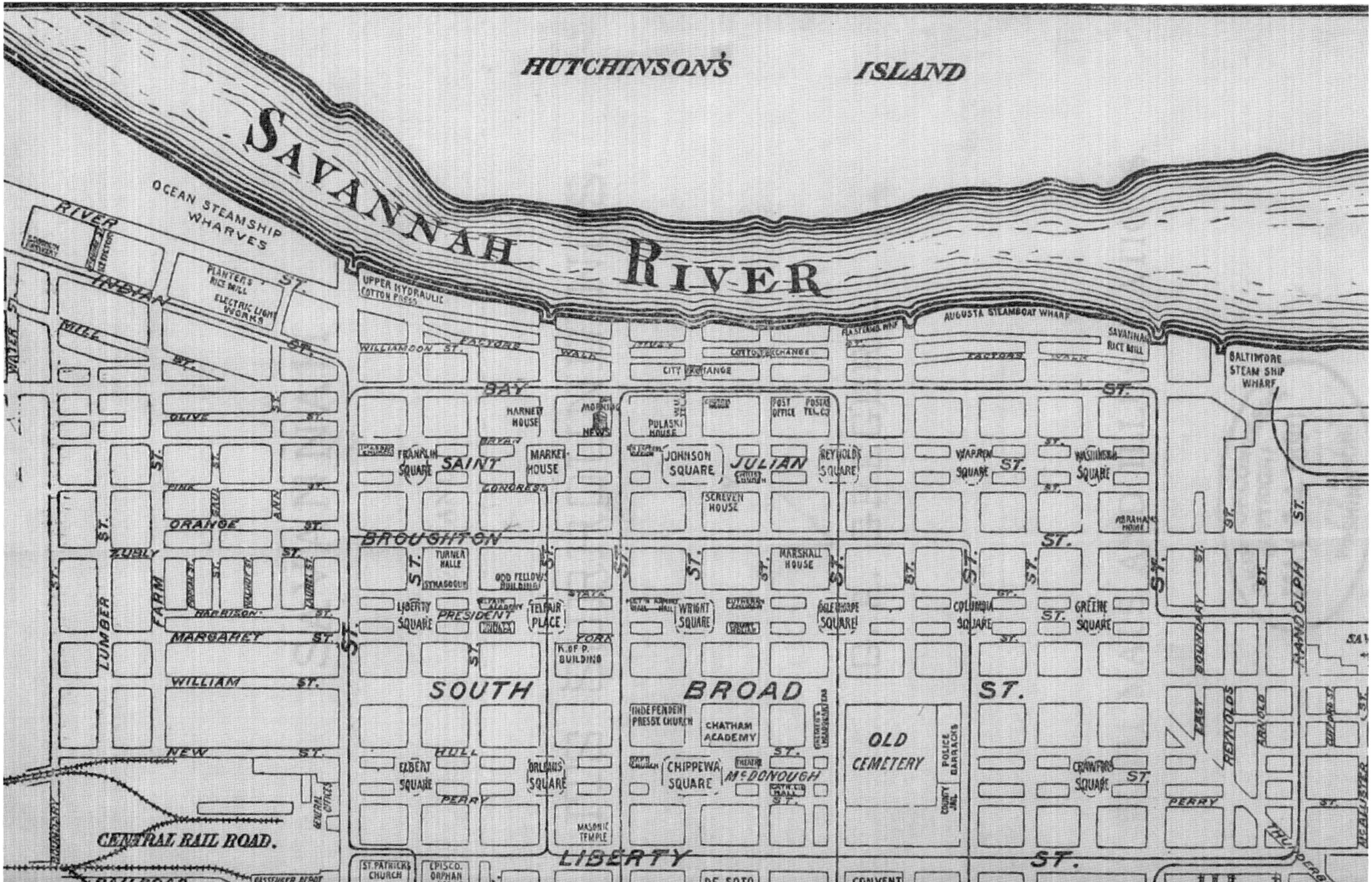
HUTCHINSON'S ISLAND
SAVANNAH RIVER
OCEAN STEAMSHIP WHARVES
RIVER
INDIAN ST.
PLANTERS RICE MILL
ELECTRIC LIGHT WORKS
UPPER HYDRAULIC COTTON PRESS
AUGUSTA STEAMBOAT WHARF
SAVANNAH RICE MILL
BALTIMORE STEAM SHIP WHARF
WILLIAMSON ST.
FACTORS WALK
CITY EXCHANGE
COTTON EXCHANGE
BAY ST.
HARNETT HOUSE
MORNING NEWS
PULASKI HOUSE
POST OFFICE
POSTAL TEL. CO.
FRANKLIN SQUARE
SAINT JULIAN ST.
MARKET HOUSE
JOHNSON SQUARE
REYNOLDS SQUARE
WARREN SQUARE
WASHINGTON SQUARE
CONGRESS
SCREVEN HOUSE
ABRAHAMS HOME
BROUGHTON ST.
TURNER HALLE
SYNAGOGUE
ODD FELLOWS BUILDING
MARSHALL HOUSE
STATE
LIBERTY SQUARE
PRESIDENT
TELFAIR PLACE
WRIGHT SQUARE
OGLETHORPE SQUARE
COLUMBIA SQUARE
GREENE SQUARE
YORK
K. OF P. BUILDING
SOUTH BROAD ST.
INDEPENDENT PRESBY. CHURCH
CHATHAM ACADEMY
OLD CEMETERY
POLICE BARRACKS
COUNTY JAIL
HULL
ELBERT SQUARE
ORLEANS SQUARE
CHIPPEWA SQUARE
McDONOUGH ST.
CRAWFORD SQUARE
PERRY
MASONIC TEMPLE
LIBERTY ST.
ST. PATRICK'S CHURCH
EPISCO. ORPHAN
DE SOTO
CONVENT
WATER ST.
MILL ST.
OLIVE
PINK
ORANGE ST.
ZUBLY ST.
FARM
LUMBER
HARRISON
MARGARET ST.
WILLIAM ST.
NEW ST.
GENERAL OFFICES
CENTRAL RAIL ROAD.
PASSENGER DEPOT
EAST BOUNDARY
REYNOLDS
ARNOLD
RANDOLPH
CLIFFORD ST.
McALLISTER
THUNDERBOLT

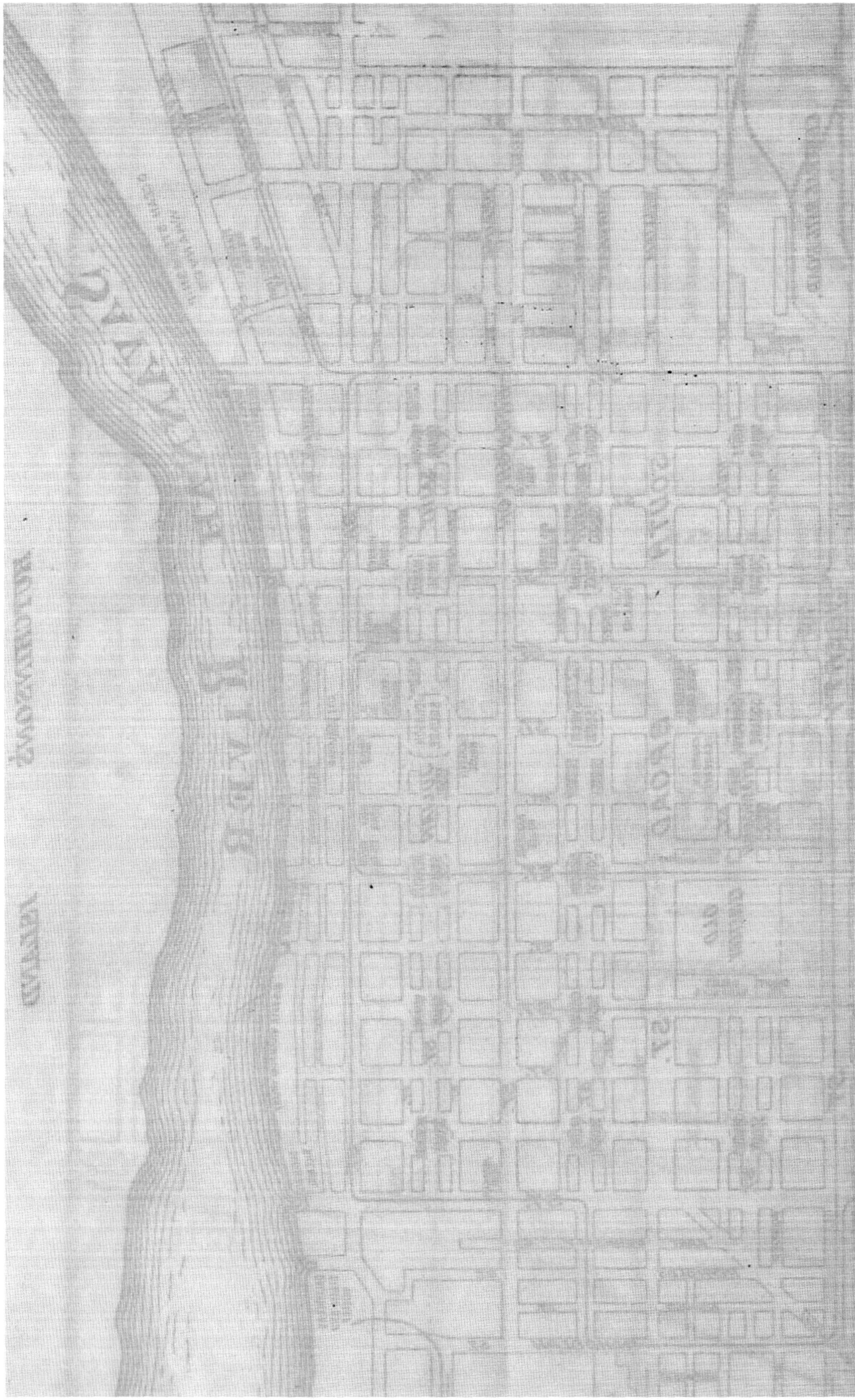

SAVANNAH

AND

ITS SURROUNDINGS.

BY

G. A. GREGORY.

WITH MAPS AND ILLUSTRATIONS.

SAVANNAH, GA.:

PRESS OF THE MORNING NEWS.

1890.

CONTENTS.

LIST OF ILLUSTRATIONS.

SAVANNAH.

THE HISTORY of Savannah began with the settlement of Georgia in 1733. In that year Oglethorpe landed on Yamacraw bluff and founded the youngest of the original thirteen colonies. There is scarcely a more romantic chapter in history than that which deals with the little colony planted upon the banks of the Savannah. Its early existence was one of privation and hardship. The difficulties and sufferings of the colonists were such that it seems marvelous that they did not abandon their new home, but they were a hardy people, and, struggling against the vicissitudes of a pioneer life, the erratic impulses of savage neighbors, and weighted with all the depressing influences of isolation, a permanent establishment was maintained. The philosophy of its foundation and fortunes belongs to the examples and facts of history.

The country South and Southwest, between the Savannah River and Florida, was, prior to 1733, a wilderness held by Indians, and claimed both by England and Spain. To secure it, Oglethorpe obtained from George II. "a grant for twenty-one years in trust for the poor," of the country between the Savannah and Altamaha Rivers, and westward to the Pacific Ocean. Oglethorpe's plan was to occupy the disputed territory by providing in it an asylum for the poor of England, and the Protestants of all nations, where former poverty would be no reproach, and where all might worship God without fear of persecution. The grant from England was the great instrument which lay at the political foundation of Georgia. Its provisions were commensurate with its design; and its privileges were as ample as the benevolence which suggested it. It gave to those over whom it stretched its fostering care the privileges of free-born Britons; the privileges of English law, and, with one exception, the privileges of religious liberty. None but those who would take the oath of transubstantiation could become colonists. Roman Catholics, consequently, were excluded, and were not admitted until Georgia became a Royal Province thirty years later.

Oglethorpe's first visit was in 1732, when he selected the site for the town and concluded a treaty with Tomo-Chi-Chi, chief of the Indian nation occupying the country. February 1, 1733, he landed with one hundred and fourteen colonists. Four tents were pitched on the bluff overlooking the river, one for each tithing, the municipal divisions into which the colonists had already been divided. This was the first occupation of Georgia and the birth of Savannah. The little settlement in time grew to the proportions of a town and was laid off with open squares and streets crossing each other at right angles. The land was divided, under a strict agrarian law, into two hundred and forty freeholds. The town land covered twenty-four square miles. Every forty houses (the houses being located on tracts of land exactly the same size) made a ward. Each ward had a constable, and under him were four tithing men. Every ten houses made a tithing; and to each tithing was a square mile divided into twelve lots. Every freeholder of the tithing had a lot, or farm of forty-five acres.

Not long after the colony was founded the religious persecutions in Germany began. The Salzburgers were driven out, and they sought new homes in Georgia. Oglethorpe and his people generously welcomed the little band of Protestants who sought their protection and their freedom of conscience. A settlement twenty miles west of Savannah on the banks of the river was assigned to them, and they called it Ebenezer in commemoration of their final deliverance from their enemies. The exile of the Salzburgers is one of the most stirring incidents of the civil and religious history of Germany, and the little settlement at Ebenezer is to-day one of the most revered places among the Lutherans of this country.

Two years later John and Charles Wesley arrived, and the founder of Methodism preached his first sermon in America in Savannah. The mission of the Wesleys proved, however, unfortunate and brief. Their religious zeal outran discretion and they were soon embroiled in conflicts with the authorities and the people, whom they did not understand. Both returned to England before they had been in America two years. The next year George Whitefield arrived, and having more tact than the Wesleys, and, from his parentage and early associations, being better fitted to cope with the rude minds of the colonists, he succeeded where they failed, and laid in Savannah the foundation of his subsequent reputation. His great work was the founding of the Bethesda Orphan House.

Hardly had the town been laid out before a colony of Israelites arrived. True to their ancient faith, they no sooner landed than they founded a synagogue, to which they gave the name Mickva Israel.

At the end of the first decade of its existence, when Oglethorpe left America finally for England, Savannah had grown to a village of three hundred and fifty houses. The government of Oglethorpe had been military, but after his departure it devolved upon the trustees in England. The colony, never very strong, languished under their chimerical views and injudicious management. Agriculture did not flourish, commerce was not thought of, silk culture, which Oglethorpe had tried to establish, failed, the colonists were deserting to Carolina and the other American possessions or were returning home, and at last in 1752, the trustees, in

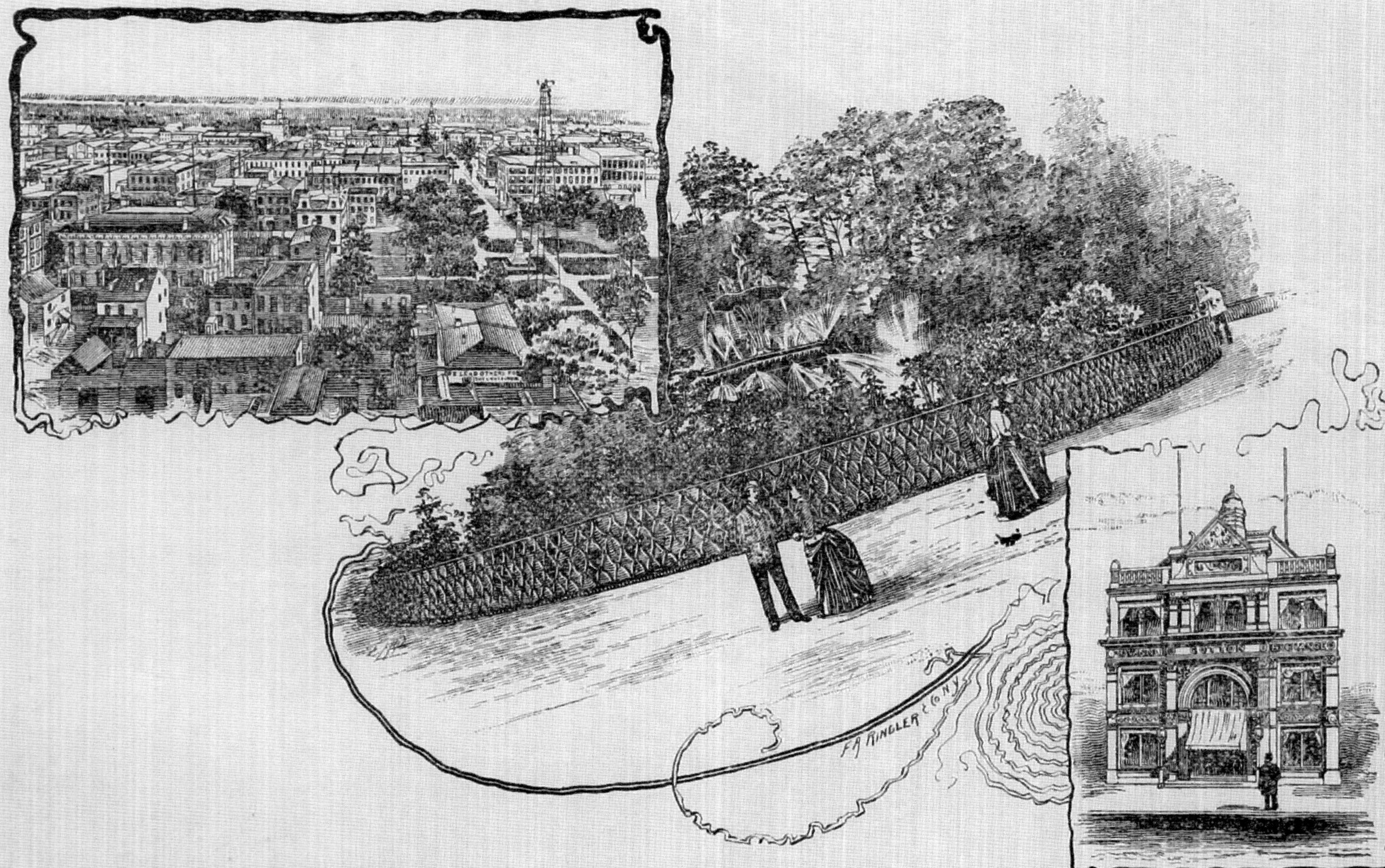

BIRD'S EYE VIEW OF SAVANNAH. FOUNTAIN IN PARK. THE COTTON EXCHANGE.

despair, resolved on account of their utter inability to support the colony, to make an absolute surrender of the charter. The resolution was carried into effect, and Georgia became a Royal Province. Under the more liberal and the wiser protection and patronage of the crown, Savannah survived and became in time the prospering foster-mother of Georgia.

Among the early excitements of Savannah was the trouble with the Spaniards in Florida, which finally culminated in open war. Spain, with her wonted arrogance, had firmly bidden the Georgians quit their newly established homes; but Spanish bravado did not frighten them. Anglo-Georgian and Hispano-Floridian fortified against each other; the same Spanish intrigue, which was at work among the thousands of negroes in South Carolina, was active among the Indians of Georgia. When at last England and Spain went to war, Oglethorpe and his colonists played an important part. They penetrated to the very walls of St. Augustine, but did not succeed in taking it.

The colonists were naturally an independent people, and the "Stamp Act" put the same fever into their blood that stirred the pulses of their cousins in Massachusetts. It is curious to note, in view of later events, that Savannah sent to the Old Bay State much of the powder used in the defense of Bunker Hill.

Although the last settled of the original thirteen colonies, neither Georgia or her chief city were backward in accepting the issues of the Revolution. A Georgia schooner was the first commissioned American vessel, and made the first capture of the war off Tybee—16,000 pounds of powder. Savannah revolted against its royal Governor early in 1776, and imprisoned him; the next year the convention which framed the State Constitution met here. Toward the close of 1778, the British, after a savagely disputed battle, captured the city; a brutal soldiery shot and bayonetted many citizens in the streets and imprisoned others on board the English ships. British rule, with all the rigor of military law, was enforced until an evacuation was rendered expedient by the success of American arms elsewhere.

There is one picture which the memory of Savannah's trials during the Revolution brings to mind—a picture which has in it the sparkle of French color, and which is a noble memorial to French gallantry and generosity. In the dull and dreadful days of 1779, when English rule had become all but intolerable, a superb fleet, one day in September, anchored off Tybee, and the amazed English saw the French colors displayed above twenty ships of the line and sixteen frigates, commanded by Count D'Estaing, sent by the King of France to aid the struggling Americans. Five thousand of the best soldiers of the French army, united with such as the American Government could muster, laid vigorous siege to the town; troops were landed and the combined forces attacked the British positions; a strong bombardment was kept up for some time, and an assault was made on the town on the 9th of October, but the besiegers were finally compelled to withdraw, leaving the city to the mercies of the enraged English. In this long and brave assault, which lasted nearly two months, the chivalrous Pulaski sealed his devotion to liberty with his life on the spot where the Central Railroad passenger depot now stands. Near by fell the gallant Jasper, who had repeatedly illustrated his valor in the cause of the colonies. The city was evacuated shortly before the close of hostilities. The exiled citizens returned, ousted the interlopers, who had acquired the traffic of the town by protection of the enemy, repaired the damages that war had wrought, to resume once more with ardor their pursuits, and to enjoy the relaxations of peace.

Savannah was, in its early history, one of the most patriotic of American towns. It not only produced men renowned for bravery and true chivalric qualities, but the people took every occasion to demonstrate their faith in the Union. The new President, Washington, was received with joyous enthusiasm. Lafayette was given an overwhelming welcome, and, during his visit, he laid the corner-stones

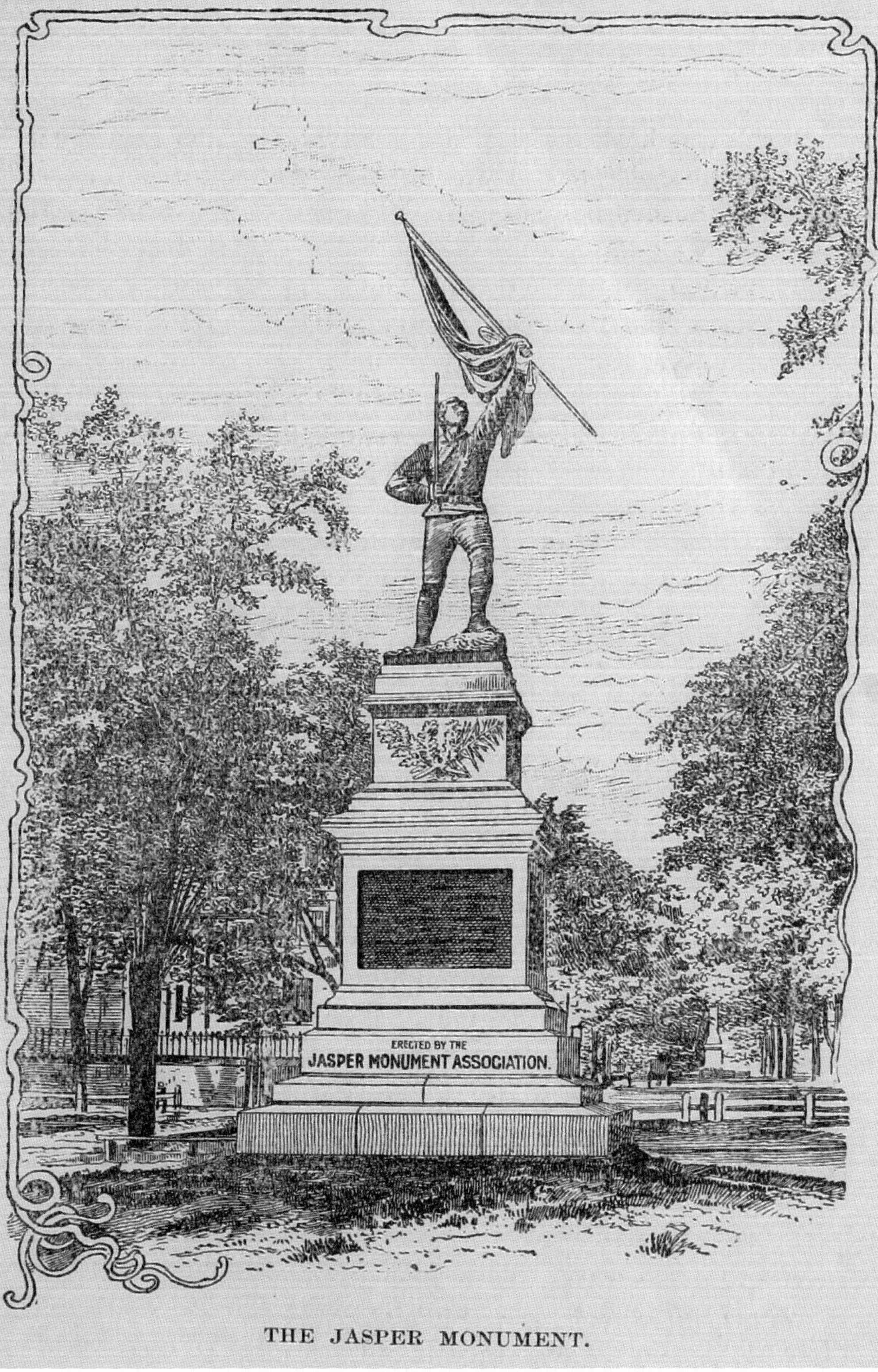

THE JASPER MONUMENT.

of two handsome monuments, which are to-day counted among the city's treasures—those to Pulaski and General Greene.

In the war between the States Savannah was the key to the Georgia coast, and it was closely watched by the Federal forces. The ordinance of secession was framed in Savannah, and it was here that the flag of the Confederate States was first hoisted in Georgia. The port was closed to commerce from 1861 to 1865. The most important events of the war occurring in the vicinity were the capture of Fort Pulaski, April 10, 1862, and the reduction of Fort McAllister, December 12, 1864. Pulaski, situated so as to command both channels of the entrance-way from the sea, had been built with great care, and it was believed to be impregnable, but rifled cannon, then a novelty in warfare, and the superior resources of the Federal forces, accomplished its surrender in twenty-seven hours. After the fall of Pulaski there were numerous encounters on land and sea, but there was no general engagement of the hostile armies until Sherman invested the city, December 11, 1864, after his famous "march to the sea," with 60,000 infantry, 6,000 cavalry, and numerous batteries of siege guns. Along the coast was a fleet of ironclads, and other war vessels, awaiting the establishment of communication with Sherman's forces to co-operate with him in the siege. Opposed to these General Hardee had, within the city and its defenses, 10,000 men. Fort McAllister had withstood three attempts to silence it and it had to be taken. Sherman cautiously enveloped the defenses of the city so as to completely isolate the fort, and then sent nine regiments to take it. The fort was held by a garrison of 150 men. It was captured after a desperate fight and through the superiority of overwhelming forces. The capture of McAllister was the conquest of Savannah. The city was evacuated December 20, 1864, and was formally surrendered the next day. Sherman's regimé, although brief, was rigorous in the extreme. Shortly after the fall of the city Lee and Johnston surrendered, and the war ended. Savannah's progress since then has not been less remarkable than that of the whole State.

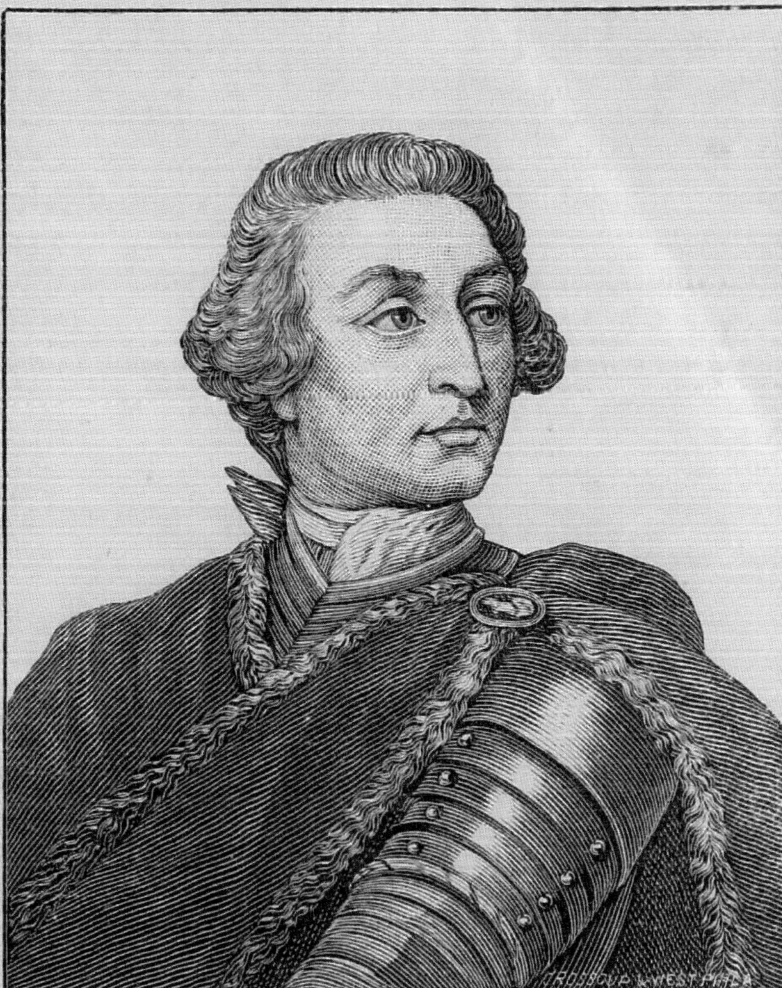

JAMES EDWARD OGLETHORPE.

James Edward Oglethorpe, the founder of Savannah, was born in London, December 21, 1688. At the age of sixteen he was admitted a student of Corpus Christi College, but did not finish his studies, war having more charms for him than literary pursuits. His first commission was that of ensign. After the death of Queen Anne he entered the service of Prince Eugene. He was elected to Parliament at the age of twenty-four, and continued a member thirty-two years. He established the colony at Savannah in 1733. In 1743 he returned to England. He was offered the command of the British forces in America operating against the Americans under Washington, but declined to accept it. He was soon afterward placed in command of an army operating against the forces of Charles the Pretender. His Christian forbearance toward the unfortunate followers of the Stuarts caused him to be charged with sympathy with their cause. A court-martial declared the charges groundless and malicious, and Oglethorpe's prosecutor was dismissed from the service. In 1744 Oglethorpe was appointed one of the field officers under Field Marshal, the Earl of Stair, to oppose the invasion of the French. He died in England, July 1, 1785.

SAVANNAH AS IT IS.

IN 1890 Savannah has a population of 60,000. The city covers 4,000 acres, and has a valuation of nearly $40,000,000 and a commerce of $110,000,000. It has 106 miles of streets, sixty-five acres of public parks, fifteen miles of street railway and five miles of wharves. Geographically, it is at the head of ship navigation on the Savannah River, eighteen miles from the ocean, on a plateau fifty feet above the level of the sea. It is in 32° and some minutes north latitude, with the gulf stream just issuing from the tropics at no great distance to the eastward. It is near the isothermal line of 70° temperature, which marks the northern limit of the tropics. The city is nearly square, and most of the streets are broad and run at right angles with each other. The plan of the city proper was designed by Oglethorpe, and once commenced it was adhered to for its regularity, beauty, and comfort. All of the streets in the city are named, and the lanes take the name of the street north of them. The plan of the outskirts differs materially from that of the city proper. Bay street is the great commercial thoroughfare, and is lined with mercantile houses, banks, and business offices. The Custom-House, the City Exchange, Post-Office, and the Cotton Exchange are on "The Bay." Congress and Broughton are the principal retail business streets. Bull street is the great promenade, and extends from the City Exchange, overlooking the river, to the park, and beyond to the southern limits and the White Bluff shell road. It received its name from Colonel William Bull, who assisted Oglethorpe in laying out the city. The street passes through five squares, in which are the Greene, Gordon, Jasper, and Pulaski Monuments, and leads to the main entrance of the park. It is the most picturesque street in the city. Upon it are some of Savannah's handsomest residences and gardens, and most imposing public buildings. Liberty and South Broad streets, the latter the original southern limit of the city, with their three and four rows of magnificent oaks interlacing their foliage and forming almost an arched avenue on either side of a broad grass plat, are two of the finest residence streets.

Forsyth Park, almost in the heart of the city, was laid off in 1853. Its plan is similar to that of the Grand Park in the City of Mexico. The park proper contains ten acres with an addition of twenty acres, used by the military as a parade ground. The main entrance is from Bull street by a broad avenue guarded by sphinxes. In the center of the park is a magnificent fountain designed from the model which was awarded the prize in the first International Exhibition in London in 1844, and similar to the grand fountain in the Place de la Concorde in Paris. Radiating from the fountain in all directions are broad, winding walks. The park is filled with trees, and their foliage is one of its chief charms. The walks are bordered with lawns, and clumps of roses, coleas, cacti and ivy and climbing plants grow luxuriantly among the native pines. In the center of the parade ground, or park extension, stands the Confederate monument.

To the fortunate early arrangement of the town by Oglethorpe, Savannah owes much of its beauty to-day. No other American city has such wealth of foliage, such charming seclusion and such sylvan perfection, so united with all the convenience and compactness of a great commercial city. The squares which were originally intended as places of refuge for the colonists, in time of attack, are now the

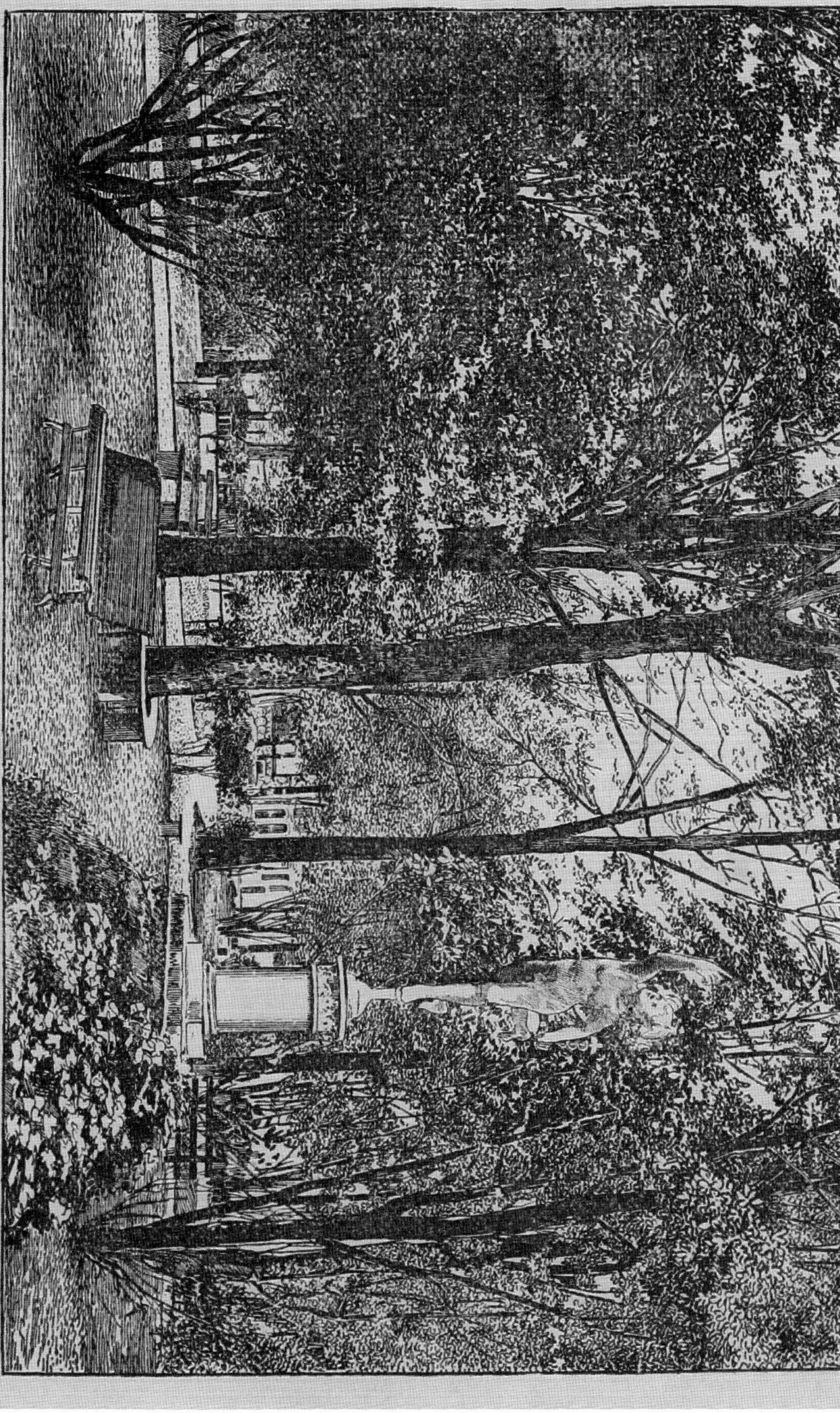

lungs of the city—the breathing spots and play grounds for children. Many of the squares are adorned with statues, fountains and mounds, gigantic oaks and magnolias, with here and there catalpas and banana trees. Among the flowers the most beautiful are the rose and the camelia-japonica which bloom luxuriantly in mid-winter in the open air.

But its natural beauty is not all that Savannah boasts. Its architecture is varied and striking; much of it in the quaint fashion of by-gone days, but with those characteristics that the art of the present day is eager to counterfeit. It is rich in historic memories; its schools are unsurpassed; its society is cultured; art is patronized, and all the influences exist which make the city attractive.

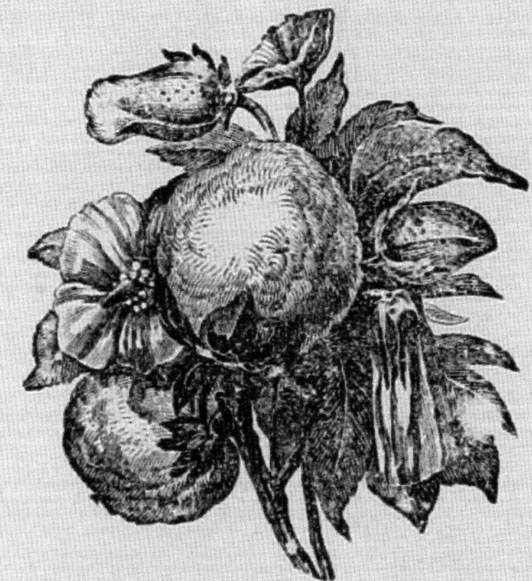

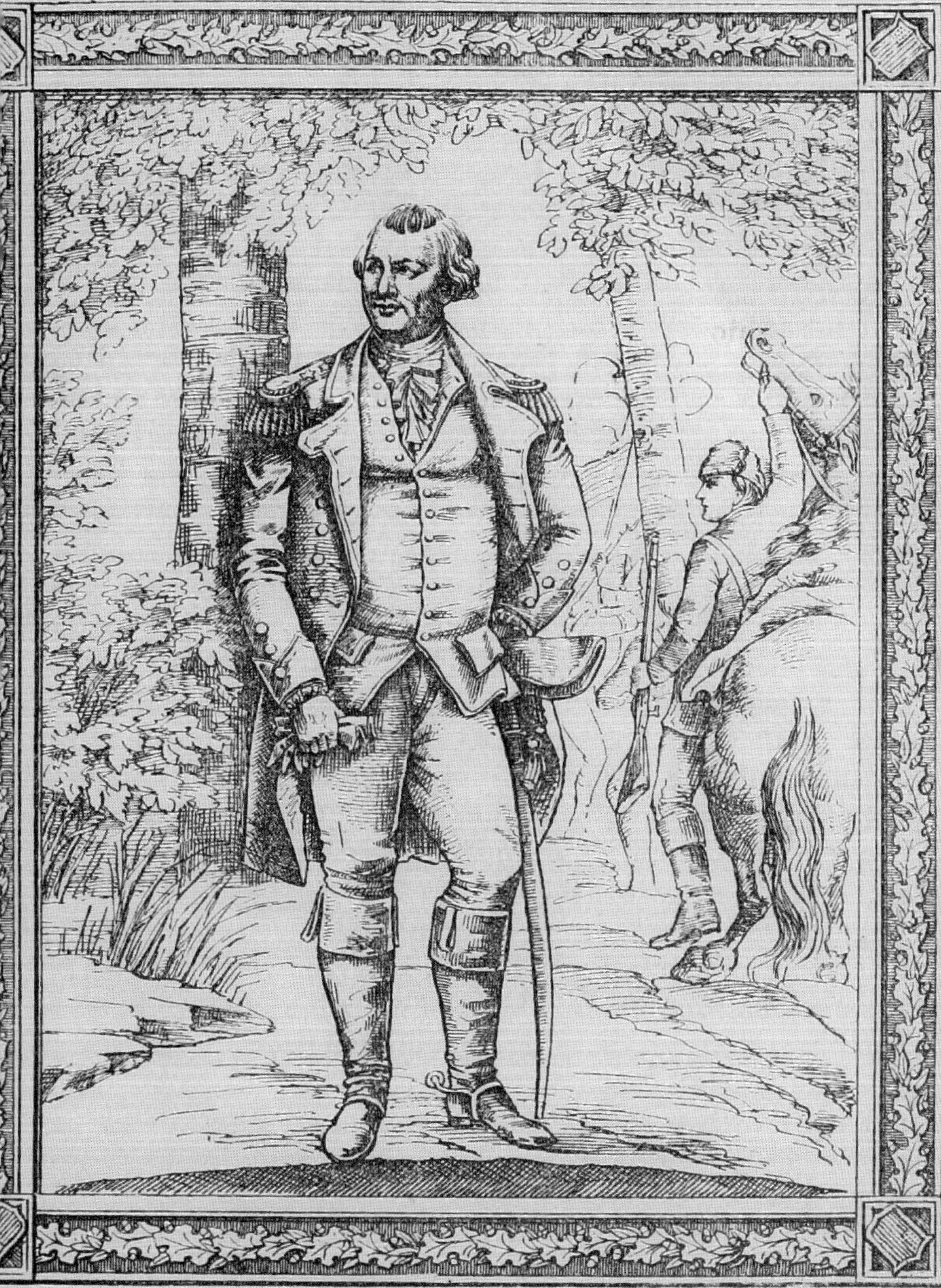

GENERAL NATHANIEL GREENE.

THE GREENE MONUMENT.

In 1825 the Marquis de Lafayette visited Savannah and laid the corner stone for two monuments—one in Chippewa square, to be erected in honor of Count Pulaski, and one in Johnson square to commemorate the eminent services to the South of General Greene. The Greene monument was finished, except the inscription, in 1829. The fund was not then sufficient to erect the monument to Pulaski, and the shaft in Johnson square was known for many years as "the Greene and Pulaski monument," in commemoration of Lafayette's visit, as well as in memory of the heroic dead, whose military careers and reputations are intimately associated with the history of Savannah. In 1886 a bronze inscriptional tablet was placed on the north face of the monument, and on the south face an *alto relievo* portrait of General Greene, in bronze. The unveiling of the tablets was a part of the centennial celebration of the Chatham Artillery. Hon. Jefferson Davis, who was a guest of the city at the time, was present and took part in the ceremonies.

In the war of the Revolution General Greene won undying fame in the Southern campaigns, and as a mark of appreciation of his services the Georgia Legislature granted him a large tract of land near Savannah. He settled upon this tract, known as Mulberry Grove, in 1783. He died in 1786 from a sunstroke, and his remains were buried with military honors in the old burying ground on South Broad street. The vault in which the remains were placed was not designated, and when, in 1820, a search was made for them they could not be found. Their resting place is to-day unknown. Tradition says that the remains were buried in the vault of the Graham family, which having been dispossessed of its lands and rights, owing to the disloyalty of Governor Graham, secretly removed the body and buried it in an unmarked spot.

THE PULASKI MONUMENT.

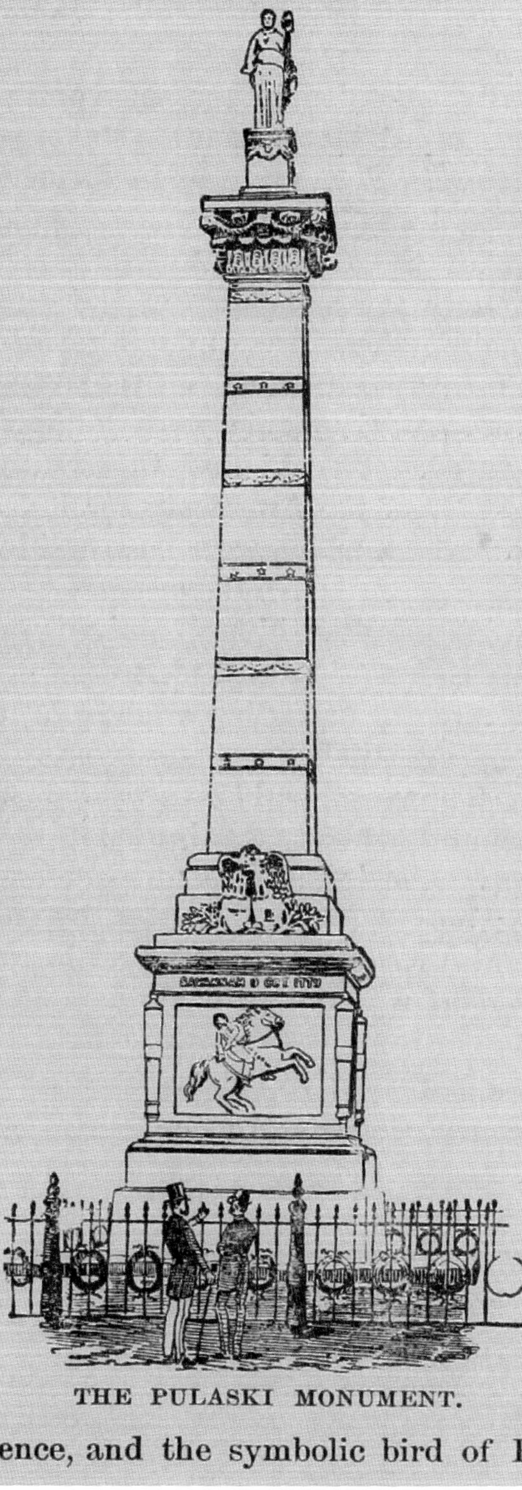

THE PULASKI MONUMENT.

The Pulaski monument in Monterey square, in memory of Brigadier-General Count Casimer Pulaski, is the last work of the famous German sculptor, Launitz. The corner stone of the monument was laid in Chippewa square in 1825, with the corner stone of the Greene monument, but was removed to Monterey square in 1853. The monument is of Italian marble and is about fifty feet high and surmounted by a statue of Liberty holding the banner of the "Stars and Stripes." It is seen at a glance that the monument is intended for a soldier who is losing his life while fighting; wounded, he falls from his horse still grasping his sword. The date, October 9, 1779, is recorded above the subject. The coats of arms of Poland and Georgia, surrounded by branches of laurel, ornament the cornice on two sides, while the eagle, emblem of liberty, courage and independence, and the symbolic bird of Poland and America, rests upon both. The reversed cannon on the corners of the die are emblematic of military loss and mourning, and give the monument a strong military character.

Count Pulaski fell mortally wounded in the siege of Savannah near the spot now occupied by the Central Railroad passenger depot. He was born in 1746, and was leader of a band of patriots confederated to relieve their native land from Russian oppression. In the struggle Austrian and Prussian troops were hurried to the assistance of the Russian forces in Poland. Against these overwhelming odds, Pulaski and his little band bravely contended, but they were overpowered and the severest punishments were inflicted upon those who were captured. Pulaski fled to France. There he learned of the struggle of the Americans for independence and tendered his services, which were accepted by Congress, and the rank of Brigadier-General was conferred upon him. After having distinguished himself in several engagements he resigned his commission and organized the famous "Pulaski Legion." After he had fallen wounded by a cannon shot in the battle of Spring Hill he was placed on a vessel to be sent to Charleston. The vessel had hardly sailed out of the harbor before he died and his body was buried at sea. There is a tradition that he was buried at Greenwich, about three miles from Savannah; but an account written by one of Pulaski's staff, who was also wounded and was on board the vessel, says that he died at sea and his body was consigned to the depths. The funeral services were held in Charleston, where the death of the brave Pole caused, as it did throughout the American colonies, the most intense grief.

THE JASPER MONUMENT.

The Jasper Monument and statue, in Madison Square, is one of the finest monuments in Savannah. It was erected by the Jasper Monument Association. The corner-stone was laid October 9, 1879, the centennial anniversary of Sergeant Jasper's death, in the siege of Savannah. The monument was completed and unveiled February 22, 1888, President Cleveland taking part in the ceremonies. The base of the monument and the pedestal are of granite. The bronze statue of Jasper, which surmounts the pedestal, is fifteen feet high and represents a sturdy specimen of manhood. The left hand clutches at arm's length a battle-worn banner. The right hand, holding an upturned sabre, is pressed tightly over a bullet wound in his side. The piece is strong in all its lines. On the face is an expression of intense suffering, held in subordination to a resolute purpose. The details of the work are clear. The fatal bullet-hole is plainly seen; upon the ground is the soldier's bullet-riddled hat, and his hair is waving in the smoke of battle. The most artistic part of the statue is the ragged banner fluttering in the wind. The statue was designed by the celebrated sculptor, Alexander Doyle, of New York. Upon the four faces of the pedestal are bas-relief panels of bronze; that on the north side is the inscriptional tablet; on the east side is a representation of Jasper standing upon the ramparts of Fort Moultrie with the rescued colors held aloft. The picture on the south side is a representation of the scene at Jasper Spring, where the prisoners were rescued, and the west side represents Jasper's death; the surgeon is beside his prostrate form, sponging the wound in his breast, among a group of comrades with sorrowful faces.

Sergeant Jasper, it is said, was of Irish descent, his family having emigrated from Ireland some years before the Revolution, and settled in South Carolina. At the beginning of the war for independence he enlisted and gave the first proof of his gallantry in the attack of the British fleet upon Fort Moultrie in 1776. The flag-staff of the Americans had been

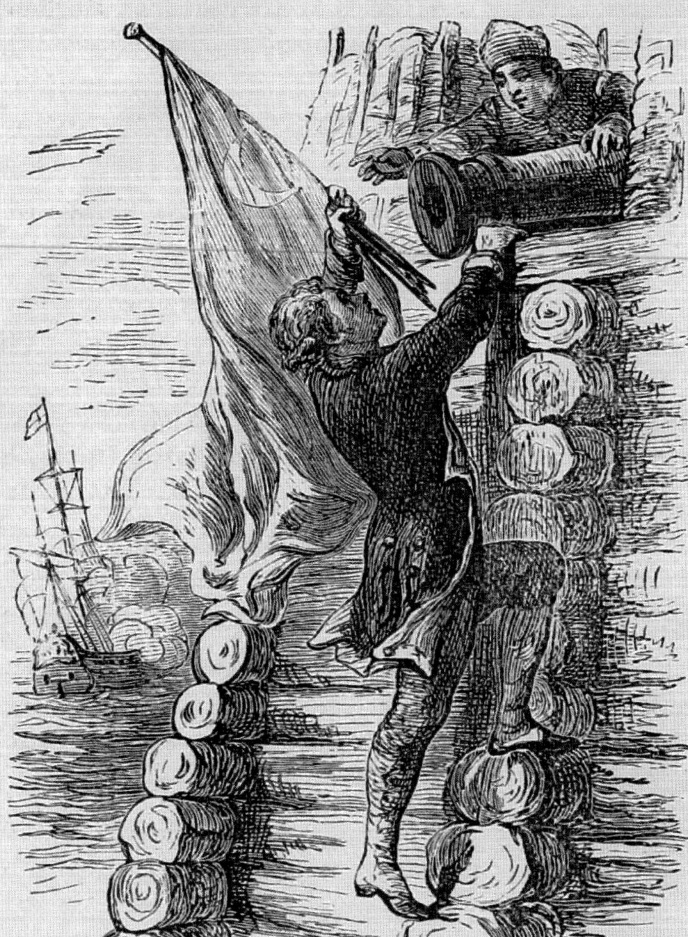

JASPER AT FORT MOULTRIE.

shot away. Jasper took up the flag, fastened it to a sponge-staff, and planted it defiantly upon the ramparts, under a heavy fire from the enemy's vessels. For this he was presented a sword and was offered a commission. He accepted the sword, but modestly declined the commission. His exploit in rescuing a number of American prisoners from a British guard, at a spring two miles from Savannah, where the party had halted for refreshment, was a daring act of cool courage. The story, as told by White in his Historical Collections, is as follows:

"Learning that a number of American prisoners were to be brought from Ebenezer to Savannah—then occupied by the British—for trial, Jasper determined to release them at all hazards. With Newton as his companion, at a spring two miles from Savannah and about thirty yards from the main road, he awaited the arrival of the prisoners. When the escort, consisting of a sergeant, corporal and eight men, and the prisoners in irons—stopped to refresh themselves at this spring, two of the guard only remained with the captives. The others leaned their guns against the trees, when Jasper and Newton sprang from their hiding place, seized the guns and shot down the two sentinels. The remaining six soldiers were deterred from making any effort to recover their guns by threats of immediate death, and were forced to surrender. The prisoners were released, and Jasper and Newton, with their redeemed friends and captive foes, crossed the Savannah River and joined the American army at Purysburgh."

The spring has been known ever since as "Jasper Spring," and is a resort of interest. It is a short distance from the Augusta road, near the Ten-Broeck race course. In the disastrous siege of Savannah by the allied American and French forces under General Lincoln and Count D'Estaing, the gallant Jasper lost his life in an attempt to replace his regimental colors within the British lines, where they had been carried by an assault. In memory of this brave, non-

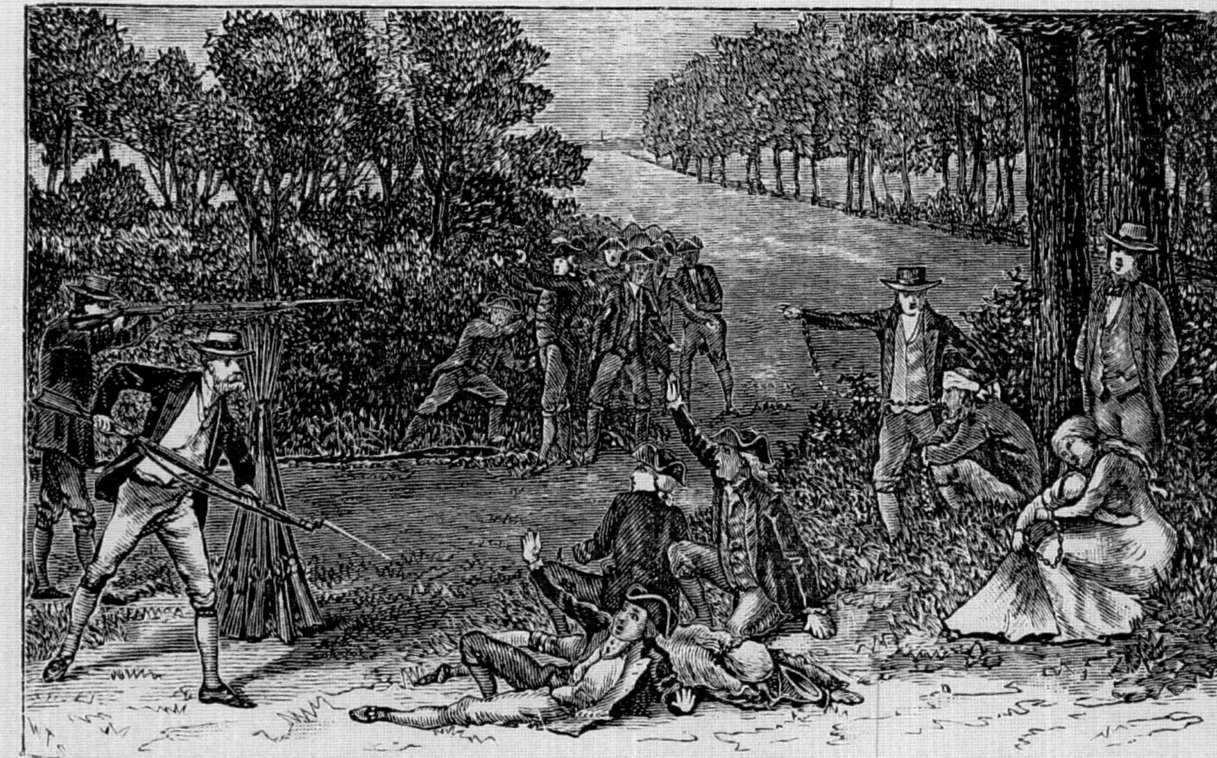

THE RESCUE AT JASPER SPRING.

commissioned officer, thus identified with the city, the monument was erected.

THE CONFEDERATE MONUMENT.

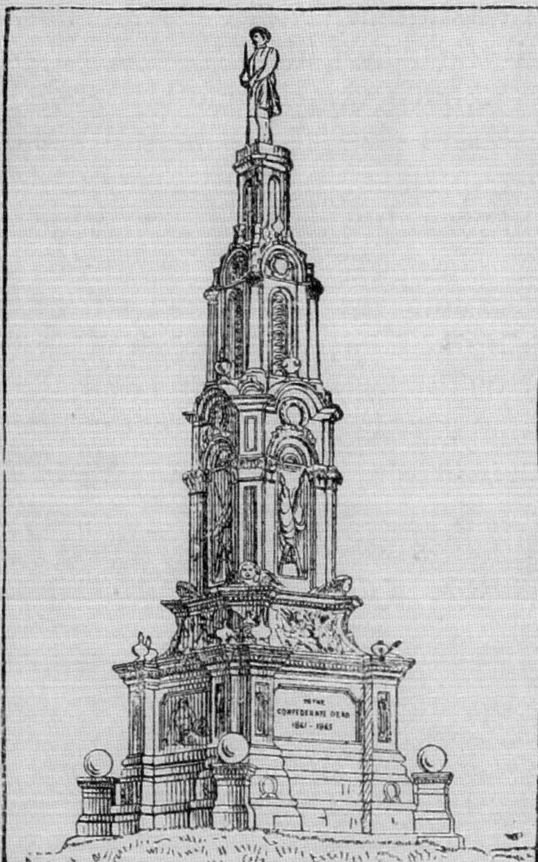

The Confederate Soldiers' monument in the parade ground was erected by the Ladies' Memorial Association to the memory of the Confederate dead. The monument stands upon a raised terrace, and is capped by a bronze statute of a Confederate soldier at "parade rest." On the die of the monument is the dedication:

"Come from the four winds,
O breath,
And breath upon these slain
That they may live."

"To the Confederate Dead,
1861–1865."

The monument was built from a design by Robert Reid, of Montreal, Canada. In style it is modern Italian. It stands about fifty feet in hight from the base to the crown of the figure by which it is surmounted. On the base of the pilasters are appropriate mottoes. The north panel on the first stage shows a figure in *alto relievo*, a prostrate woman representing the South in mourning; from her left hand she lets fall a branch of laurel. In one corner of the panel is a group of weeping willows with their drooping branches. The reverse panel is left vacant, although the design provides for its occupany by a figure, also *alto relievo*, of a military character. Above the panels is a rich cornice. The next stage was originally an open canopy supported on pilasters, underneath which was a marble statue of Silence, but this was removed and the space filled with stone to strengthen the structure. Above this is another stage, deeply recessed and moulded, and ornamented with draped banners, guns and sabres. The topmost panel is exquisitely moulded and forms the base upon which rests the crowning figure. The corner stone of the monument was laid June 16, 1875, and the monument was unveiled in May, 1876. The bronze statue is a work of art. Ease, grace and manliness distinguish the figure, and the musket, worn hat, and tattered clothing are true to the life, reproducing with wonderful exactness the rents, patches, darns and rude sewing that betray the deprivations and hardships which the Confederate soldiery had to endure in their gallant, but painful, struggle of four years of unsuccessful warfare.

THE GORDON MONUMENT.

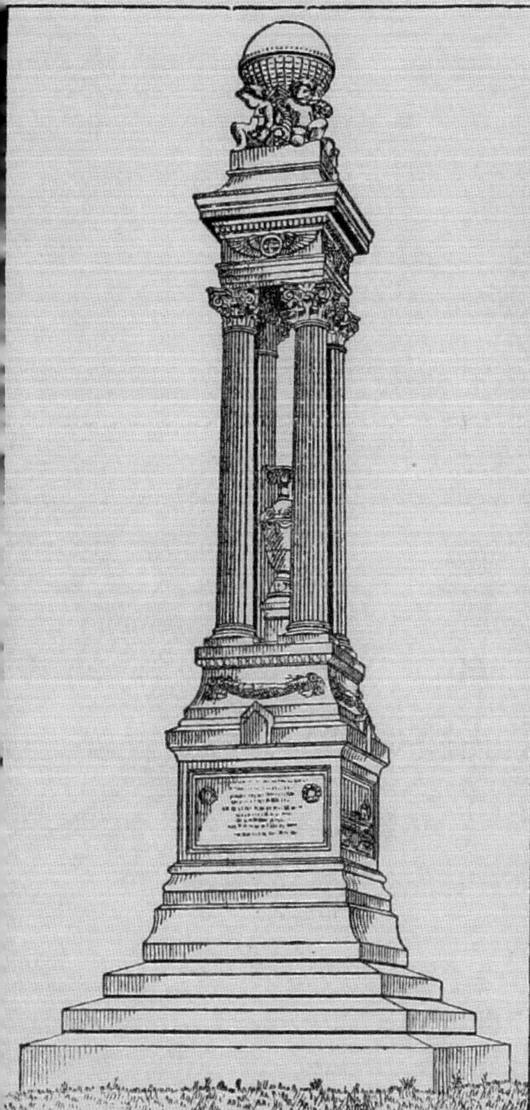

THE GORDON MONUMENT.

The Gordon monument, in Court House square, was erected in 1883 by the Central Railroad and Banking Company in memory of William W. Gordon, the first President of the road. The monument is not only a tribute to the memory of the man to whom it was erected, but it illustrates the spirit of progress and the advance of internal improvement in Georgia since the Central Railroad was inaugurated, in 1834. The design of the monument is beautiful and suggestive. The north face bears the name "Gordon." The eastern face is a bas-relief representing a locomotive and train of cars emerging from a tunnel and approaching a viaduct, beyond which, in the distance, are the tall spars of shipping. The south face bears the inscription:

In memory of
William Washington Gordon.
Born June 17, 1796.
Died March 20, 1842.

The pioneer in works of internal improvement in his native State, and President of the Central Railroad and Banking Company of Georgia, to which

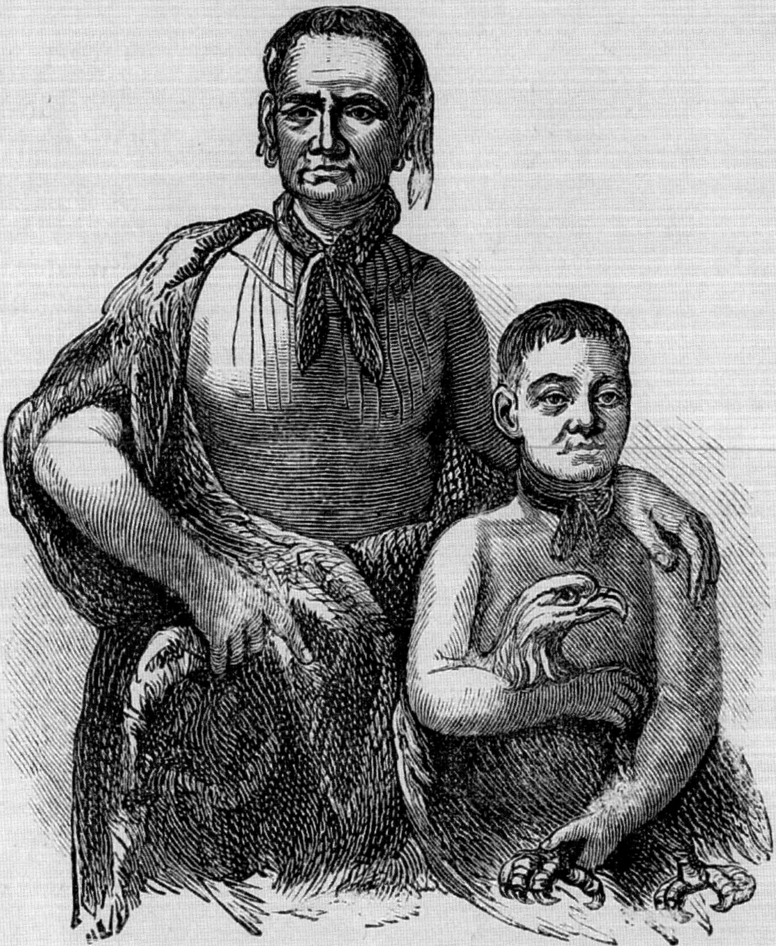

TOMO-CHI-CHI AND HIS NEPHEW.

The remains of Tomo-Chi-Chi, the famous Indian chieftain, are supposed to have been buried in Court House square, in the vicinity of the Gordon monument. Tomo-Chi-Chi died in 1738. At his own request he was buried among his friends, the white men, with the pomp and circumstance due to his high rank and staunch friendship, and within the compass of the colonists. Oglethorpe assisted as pall-bearer; the burial was in what was then Percival square. Minute guns were fired during the march of the procession, and as the body was lowered three volleys of musketry were fired over it.

THE GEORGIA HISTORICAL SOCIETY.

The Georgia Historical Society was organized in 1839. Its library, numbering 20,000 volumes, is one of the finest collections in the South. The Society was chartered "for the purpose of collecting, preserving, and diffusing information relating to the State of Georgia in particular, and of American history generally." The Georgia Medical Society is a part of the Historical Society. Hodgson Hall, the library building, at Whitaker and Gaston streets, fronting the park, was erected by Mrs. Margaret T. Hodgson and Miss Mary Telfair, the widow and sister-in-law of William B. Hodgson, in his memory. These ladies bequeathed over one-half of their large estate to the fostering and sustenance of the cause of literature, science and art in Savannah. The Historical Society, in which they felt a deep interest, has, through their liberality, been most munificently endowed. Miss Telfair, carrying out the wishes of her sister, which were in consonance with her own, bequeathed the Society the family mansion on Telfair place with all the furniture, pictures, works of art, etc., and $100,000 of railroad stock, to establish and maintain an Academy of Arts and Sciences. It is therefore not to be wondered at that the names of these ladies are held in such high esteem and reverence by the Historical Society and by the people of Savannah. The building was designed by Detlef Lienau, of New York, the architect who later designed the Telfair Academy annex. The exterior of the building is plain, its architecture being adapted to the convenience and comfort of the library. The front, however, is ornamental, being chiefly of brown stone. The entrance is by massive stone steps and portico. The frieze of the portico bears, in relief, the inscription, "W. B. Hodgson Hall." Upon the building is similarly inscribed, "Georgia Historical Society."

If the exterior is plain, the interior of the library hall is strikingly attractive. The hall contains several fine portraits of members of the Society, and of men prominent in the

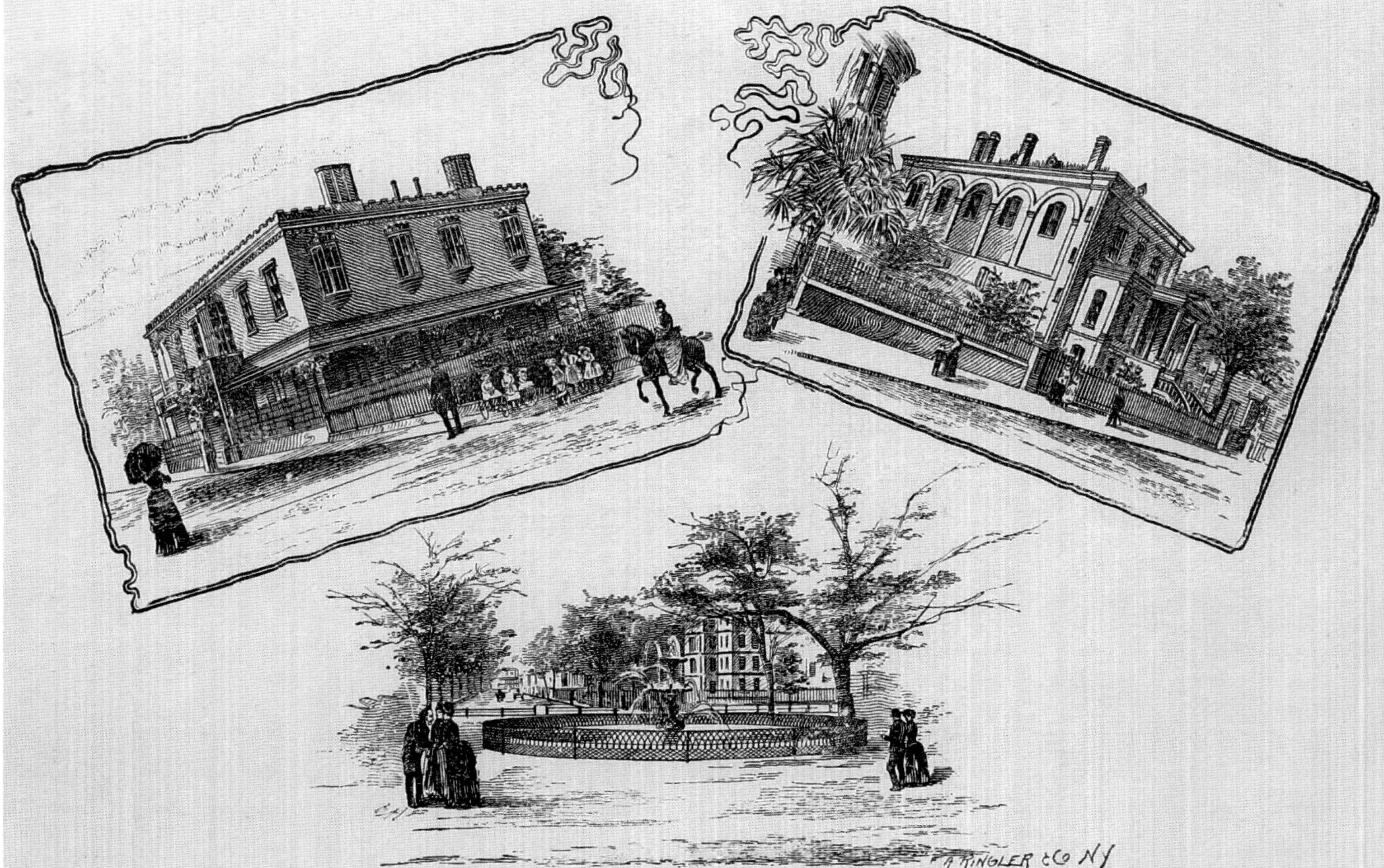

GREEN RESIDENCE. BULL STREET. GEORGIA HISTORICAL SOCIETY LIBRARY.

history of Georgia and the South, and an interesting collection of historical relics. Fronting the entrance is a platform, or rostrum. Above this is an admirable portrait of Mr. Hodgson, one of the earliest members of the Society, and for over twenty-five years one of its curators. The picture was painted by Carl L. Brandt, the present Director of the Telfair Academy. It represents Mr. Hodgson in his library, standing by a table, in the act of turning the leaves of a book. On the table are books and papers and a scroll covered with Arabic characters, symbolic of Mr. Hodgson's studies. The features, dress and attitude of the figure give a life-like appearance, and, with a brilliant light and the faithful reproduction of the appurtenances of a library, betoken the genius of the artist. Beneath the picture is a marble slab with this inscription:—

In Memory of
WILLIAM BROWN HODGSON,
this building is erected by
MARGARET TELFAIR HODGSON,
Anno Domini 1873.

The building was dedicated to the Historical Society in 1876. The library is open to members and visitors. The library hours are 10 A. M. to 9 P. M.

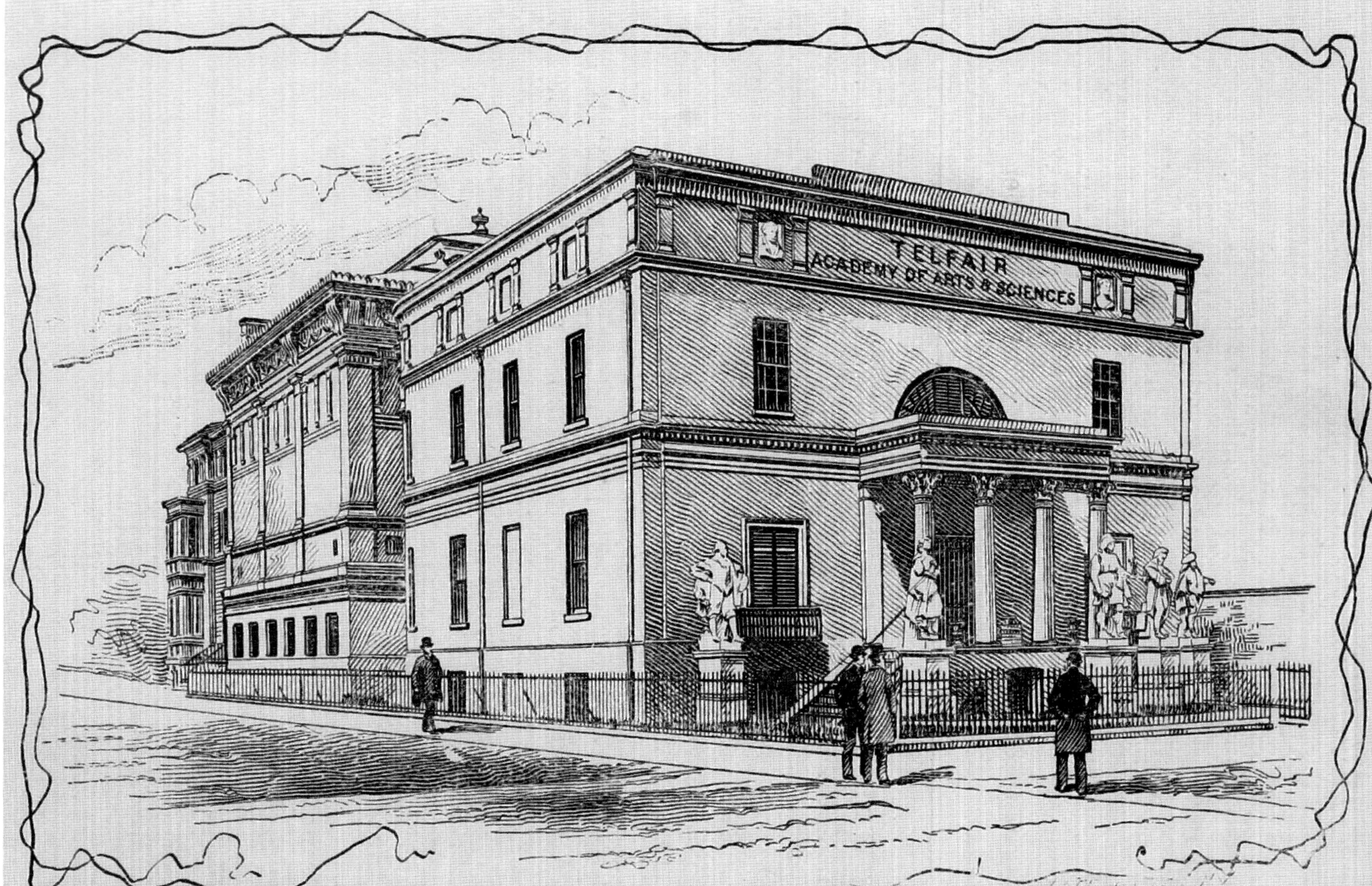
TELFAIR
ACADEMY OF ARTS & SCIENCES

THE TELFAIR ACADEMY OF ARTS AND SCIENCES.

The Telfair Academy of Arts and Sciences, on Telfair Place, is the art gallery of the South. It was founded through a bequest of Miss Mary Telfair, who, upon her death, bequeathed the Telfair family mansion and $100,000 for the purpose of founding an art museum and academy. The bequest was under the trusteeship of the Georgia Historial Society, and the Academy was opened in 1885. A writer in the Magazine of Art says that the Academy is like nothing so much as a bit of Munich strayed from the banks of the Iser to the new world. It is the Glyptothek and Pinakothek in one. In front of the building are five heroic size statues of Rubens, Raphael, Michael Angelo, Phideas and Rembrandt, modeled for the Academy by Viennese sculptors and carved in white Marzina stone. The entrance hall of the Academy is lined with photographs, forming part of a series which is continued in the large picture gallery. It includes reproductions of the masterpieces of ancient and modern art, from the best European photograph publishers. Beyond the entrance hall is a collection of plaster relief heads. The Director of the Academy is Carl L. Brandt, N. A. He is director, teacher and curator. The Academy is the embodiment of his ideas, and his classic Munich tendencies are revealed everywhere in the building, which is one of the finest bits of architecture in the country. At the left of the entrance corridor is an old room hung with old masters and copies. On the north side of the corridor is the Phideas room. Here are some of the finest of the Parthenian marbles, forming part of one of the most satisfactory collections of antique casts in the United States. The east pediment of Parthenon is here complete.

The large sculpture hall has in its center that group so seldom seen in its entirety—the "Tauro Farnese," of the Naples museum. It is the second cast ever obtained directly from the original and was made expressly for the Telfair Academy. It was shipped to America in twenty-one

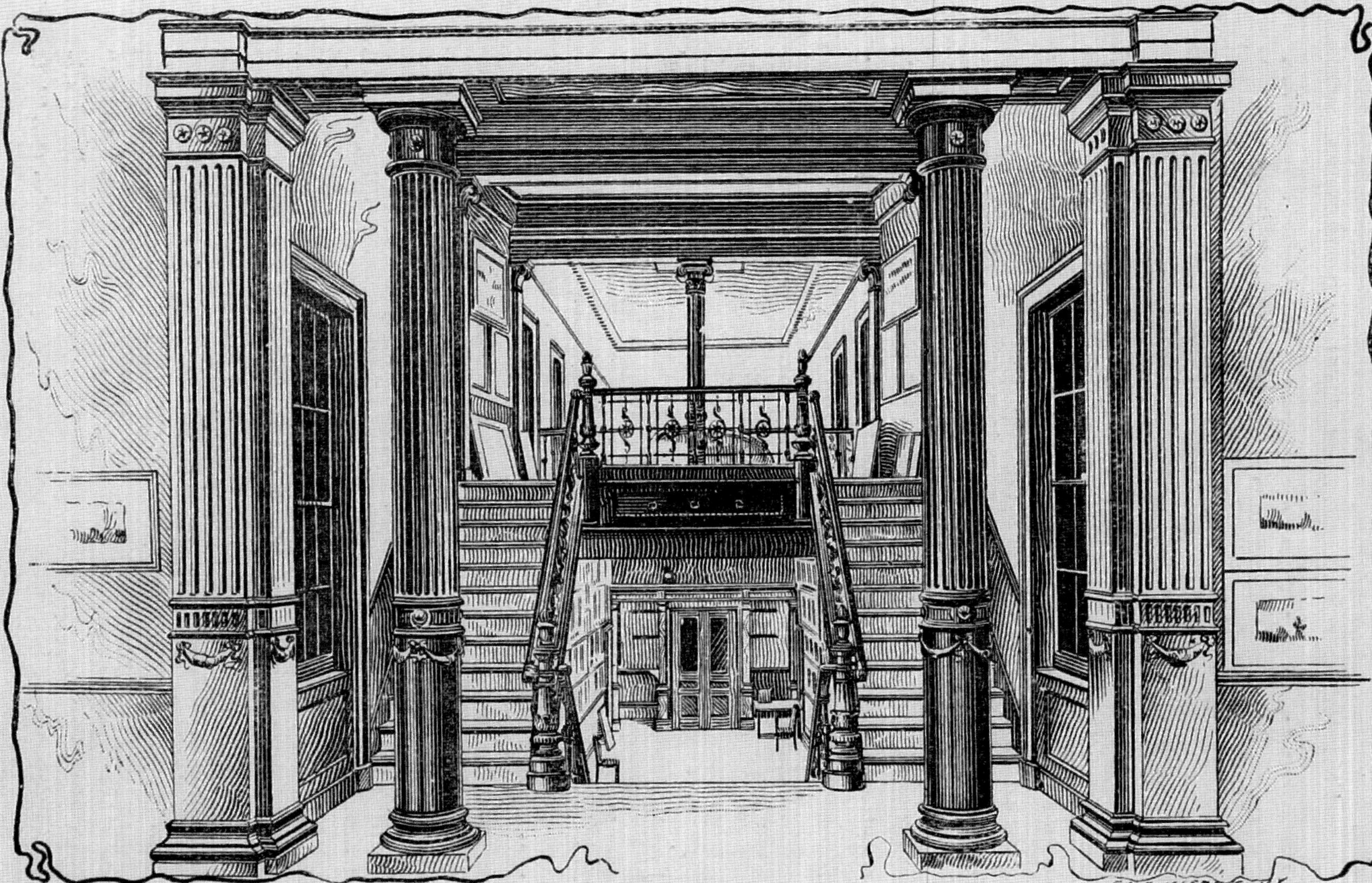

ACADEMY OF ARTS AND SCIENCES—ENTRANCE CORRIDOR.

cases, containing one hundred and twenty-six sections, and arrived broken into a thousand pieces. It required months of patient work by the director to put this monument of ancient art together, and as it stands to-day, it shows no trace of the experience through which it passed. The statuary hall also contains a fine copy of the famous Gaeta vase.

The picture gallery is a beautiful example of classic decoration; the pervading color is Pompeiian red, which is largely used throughout the building. At the top of the room, forming a wide frieze all around it, are superb mural paintings, simulating tapestries, by Director Schraudolph, of Stuttgart. They are forty-four feet in length and nine feet high, and present allegorical representations of the different arts. Among the chief pictures in the gallery are those of the Munich and Dusseldorf schools. The great picture of the gallery, both in size and masterful execution, is Kaulbach's "Peter Arbues of Epila." The picture was finished in 1870, and is the last work of the famous artist. It is sixteen feet long by thirteen feet high. "Ein Gefecht," by Josef von Brandt, a Polish artist of Munich, next to Kaulbach's, is the pride of the gallery. The picture is what its title implies—a calvary attack. It is a large canvas and occupies a place on the west wall of the gallery. The subject is a fight between the Poles and the allied Swedes and Brandenburgers in the days of the battles before Warsaw. A half destroyed village is occupied by a small detachment of the allied troops, which is attacked by a superior squadron of the "dreaded mailed Lancers," who, with furious force, fly to the combat of the ususpecting enemy. The attack of the rattling lines, the wild confusion of the hand to hand fight, is represented with most convincing truthfulness and wonderful pictorial power and art. The picture was secured from the Munich Exposition in 1888. Next to "Ein Gefecht" is Szymanowski's "Dispute of Russian Mountaineers," which was secured from the Paris Exposition in 1889. In character and literary interest "The

Relics of the Brave," by Arthur Hacker, is one of the masterpieces of the gallery. Julian Story's "The Black Prince," secured from the Paris Exposition, is one of the largest pictures, and one of the most striking.

The upper rooms of the Academy are a series of galleries. The famous Parthenon frieze surrounds the entrance hall, and in the adjoining rooms are the archæological and prehistoric art collections, arrow heads and flints, and photographs of ancient ruins and edifices. The gallery also contains an interesting collection of Japanese embroideries, bronzes and Italian wood engraving. The Academy is open to visitors daily, except Sundays, from 10 A. M. to 5 P. M. Sundays from 1 to 5 P. M.

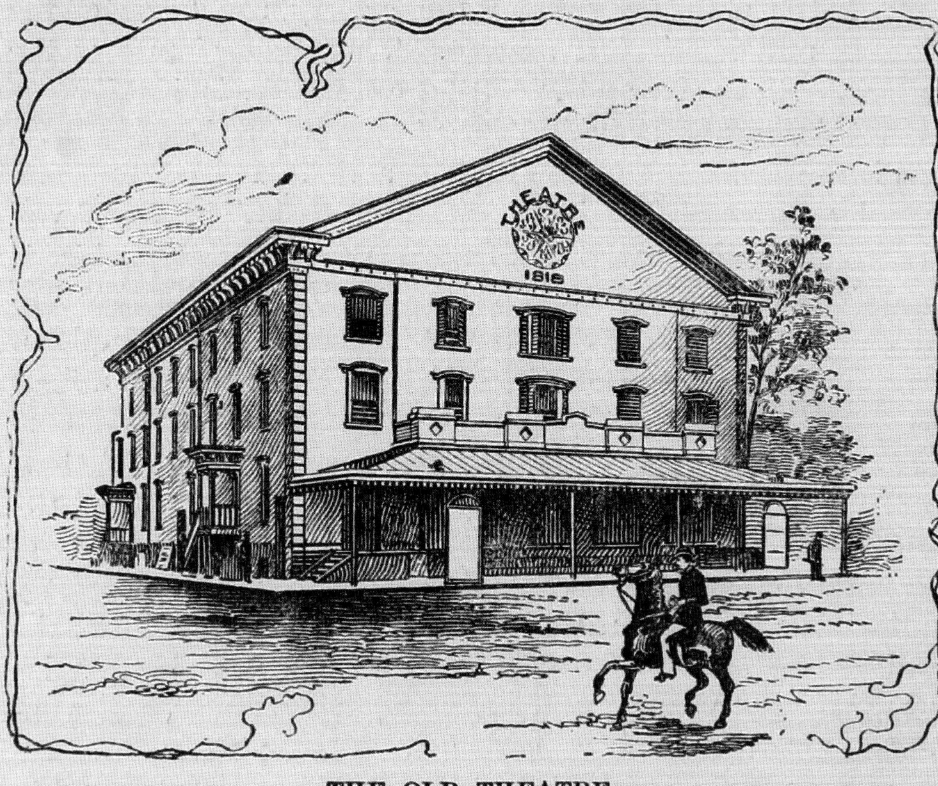

THE OLD THEATRE.

The Savannah Theatre, on Bull street, fronting Chippewa Square, is the oldest theatre in the United States. It was built in 1818, and was opened December 4th of that year, and for nearly three-quarters of a century has been the chief place of amusement in Savannah. Since it was built many changes have been made in its interior, but the exterior has undergone little change. It has witnessed the rise, progress and decadence of the drama in America. Its walls have resounded with the sonorous tones of the elder and the younger Booths, of McCready, Vandenhoff, the Kembles, father and daughter; the Coopers, Forrest, and hosts of other tragedians and melo-dramatists, and have echoed the comicalities of Finn, Hilson, the two Placides, and Hackett, and absorbed the melting tones and artistic roulades and trills of Kelly, Hughes, Russell, and the stars of operatic music. The voices of past generations and of the present are blended in the silence of its venerable walls. The history of the Savannah Theatre is a record of the stage in the United States, and critical were the audiences, in the days of the legitimate drama, which criticised the performances upon its boards.

THE CITY EXCHANGE.

The City Exchange—the city hall—at the foot of Bull street, was built in 1799, and is a type of the architecture of that time. It was built by a stock company and was intended for a Merchants' Exchange. The site was leased for ninety-nine years and the building cost $20,000. The city was a member of the company, and, by successive purchases of stock, it became, in 1812, the possessor of the property and converted it into a city hall, which it still is, though the original name, "Exchange," is retained. The lower part of the building is occupied by business offices. The second and third stories contain the Council Chamber and the various departments of the City Government. In the "Long Room" is a life-size painting of General Robert E Lee—pronounced the finest portrait of Lee extant. In the Exchange steeple are the venerable city clock and fire bell, which have hung there for more than three-quarters of a century. The old clock bears the inscription, "Built by

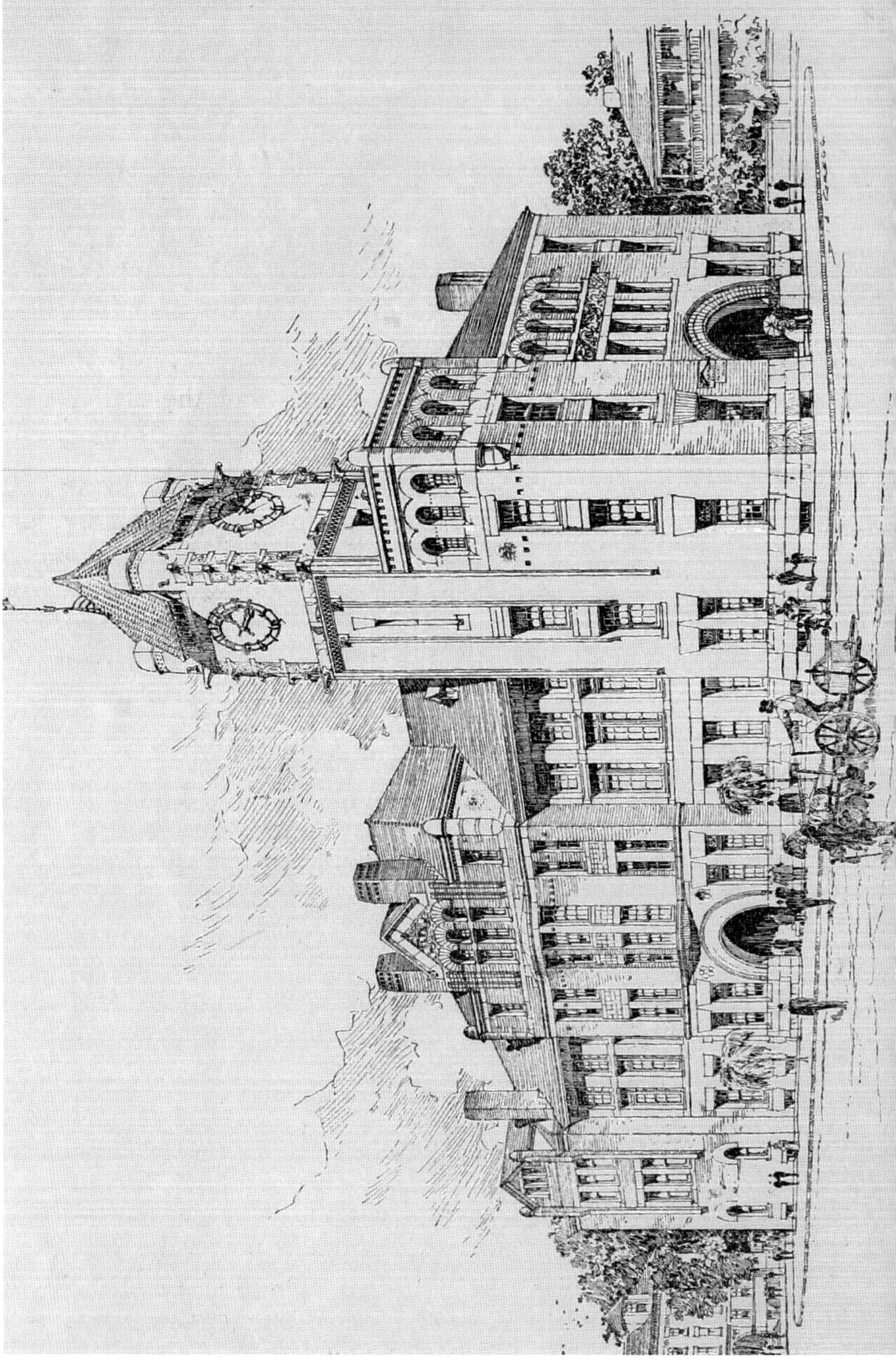

John Thwaites, Clerkenwell, London, 1803." From the steeple a splendid view of the city is obtained. Bull street, with its squares and monuments, extends south to the park, and is lined with public buildings and residences. Piercing the foliage is the tall spire of St. John's, and rising up in front, the Ionic proportions of Christ Church, and the lofty roof of the Cathedral of St. John the Baptist, are clearly seen. The visitor at once realizes the appropriateness of the title "Forest City," in its application to Savannah, as the city can scarcely be seen for the trees—only the spires, steeples, and the roofs of the houses rising above the foliage. From the balcony of the Exchange the military reviews take place, and from it Sherman reviewed the Federal army at the close of his famous "march to the sea." The "Long Room" has been the scene of many historic events. It was here, in 1886, that Jefferson Davis held his last public reception.

PUBLIC BUILDINGS AND LOCALITIES.

The County Court House, on Court House square, is one of the finest public buildings in the State. It is built upon the site of the old court house, which was demolished in 1889, and cost $160,000. The corner stone was laid July 31, 1889. The first court house was at the northeast corner of Bull street and Bay lane. Just before the Revolution a brick court house was erected upon the site of the present building. During the siege of Savannah it was occupied by the British troops as a headquarters and was damaged by shells thrown from the American and French batteries. Upon the re-occupation of the city the building was restored and was used until 1831 when it was torn down to make room for the recent structure which was completed in 1833.

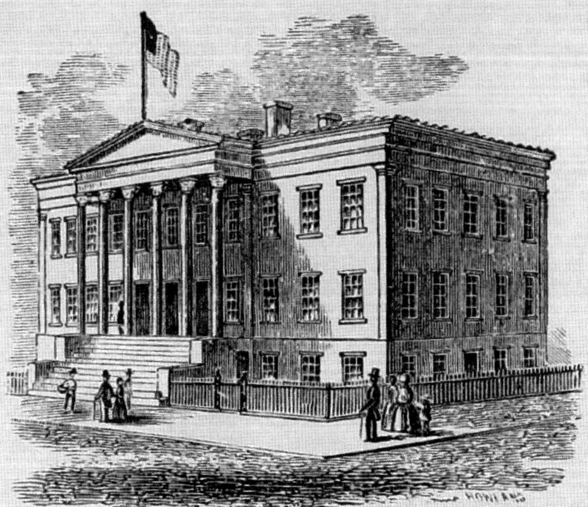

The United States Custom House, at Bay and Bull streets, contains the customs offices, Internal Revenue office, United States Marine Hospital Surgeon's office, the Branch Hydrographic office, and the United States Courts, District Attorneys and United States Marshal's and Commissioners' and Shipping Commissioners' offices and the offices of Inspectors of Steamboats. The building was erected in 1850. There is no record of the first custom house, although such a building existed as early as 1763. In 1789 the customs office was in Commerce Row west of the City Exchange. From there it was removed to a building which stood on the site of the old Georgia Historical Society building on Bryan street, and afterwards to the City Exchange until the present Custom House was built. The building is open to visitors.

The Morning News Building, on Whitaker street, is one of the largest and finest buildings in Savannah. It was erected in 1876 and was enlarged in 1886. It is six stories high, and its tower, nearly one hundred feet above the street, commands a magnificent view of the city and the surrounding country. The entire building is occupied by the Morning News Printing House.

Masonic Temple, at Liberty and Whitaker streets, was built by Solomon's Lodge No. 1, the oldest lodge of Freemasons in this country. There is little but tradition concerning the early history of Freemasonry in Georgia. The records of Solomon's Lodge previous to the Revolution of 1776 were destroyed during the occupancy of the city by the British. The present records go back to 1784. According to the records of the Grand Lodge of England the lodge was organized in 1735 under a charter from that body. Solomon's Lodge is not only the mother lodge of Georgia, which gave the present Grand Lodge its existence, but it is the oldest working body of Masons in America. Among its archives is a Bible presented by Oglethorpe.

THE ODD-FELLOWS' BUILDING, at Barnard and State streets, is on the site of the building burned in 1889. When Washington visited Savannah in 1791 he was entertained in the house that formerly occupied this site. The new building is a handsome structure, and is the meeting place of five lodges, an encampment and a uniformed canton of the order. Oglethorpe Lodge, No. 1, is the mother lodge of Odd-Fellows in Georgia. It was organized in 1842. The Grand Lodge of Georgia was organized in Savannah in 1844.

THE COTTON EXCHANGE was organized in 1872. Its building, on Bay street, at the foot of Drayton, is one of the finest in the city. Visitors are admitted to the floor of the Exchange through introduction by members.

THE BOARD OF TRADE, orgaLized as the Savannah Naval Stores Exchange in 1882, was reorganized as the Board of Trade in 1883, its original purpose and scope having been enlarged to include other branches of trade than naval stores. It is supported by the naval stores, rice, grain, flour, and provisions, and fertilizer interests.

THE CHATHAM ACADEMY, at Bull, South Broad and Drayton streets, was incorporated in 1788, and is the oldest educational institution in Georgia. The first free school in Savannah was established in 1816. The Chatham Academy building was erected by the Chatham Academy Trustees and the Union Society in 1818. In 1886 the interest of the latter was purchased and the building was remodeled. It contains the High School, the Chatham Academy Grammar School, and offices of the Superintendent of Schools and the Board of Education.

THE GREEN RESIDENCE, on Bull street, fronting Madison Square, was General Sherman's headquarters during his

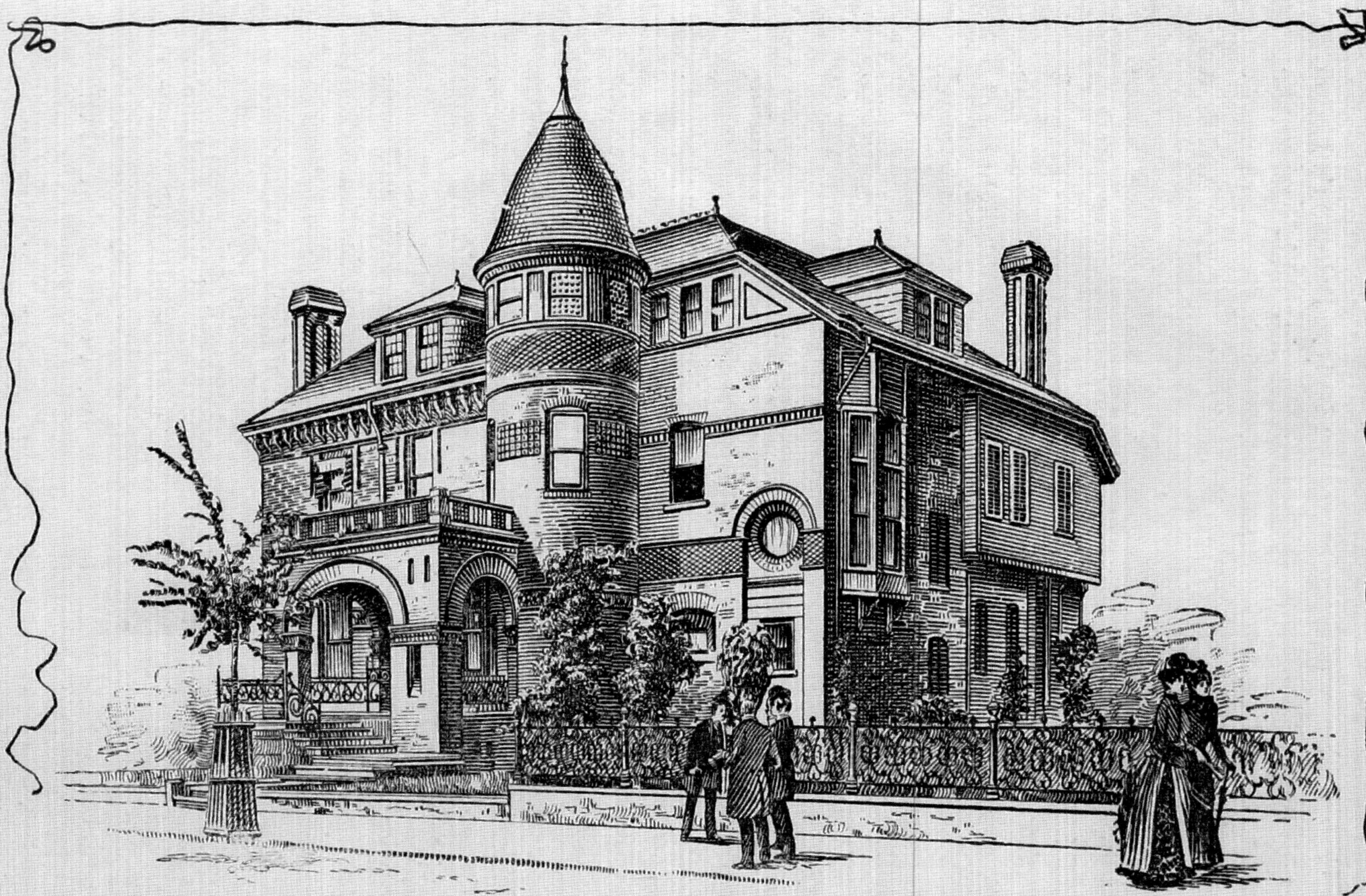

A HALL STREET RESIDENCE

occupancy of the city after the Confederate evacuation in 1864, and it has since been known as "Sherman's Headquarters." The residence is on the English style of architecture, and its occupancy by Sherman has made it a point of historical interest.

THE PUBLIC MARKET, in Market Square, is to strangers a point of special interest. The market building covers an entire square. It was built in 1872. The roomy basement, half underground, and the market above it, are the great food supply center of the city. A Saturday night visit to the Market affords one of the most interesting sights in Savannah.

THE POLICE BARRACKS, at South Broad and Habersham streets, is the headquarters of the Police Department. The building contains the Police Court-room, officers' quarters and barracks-rooms, and City Jail. It was erected in 1868.

THE COUNTY JAIL, on Habersham street, south of the Police Barracks, was built in 1887 at a cost of $50,000. It is of brick and iron, with iron cells, and Sheriff's residence.

THE COTTON COMPRESSES are among the principal objects of interest to visitors. The Gordon presses are at the Ocean Steamship Company's wharves, and the Upper Hydraulic Presses are at the foot of Montgomery street. A bale of uncompressed cotton averages 38¼ cubic feet, with an average of 12⅗ pounds per cubic foot. After the bale has been compressed it averages 18 cubic feet, with an average of 28 pounds per cubic foot. The pressure in compressing a bale is from 1,500 to 2,000 tons. In no city in this country has the attention been paid to compressing cotton that there is in Savannah.

THE RICE MILLS of Savannah are interesting, from the fact that, except those in South Carolina and Louisiana, they are the only mills in this country. There are three mills—the Upper Mills, on River street, near Farm; the Planters' Mill, on River street, near Ann, and the Savannah Mill, on River street, at the foot of East Broad.

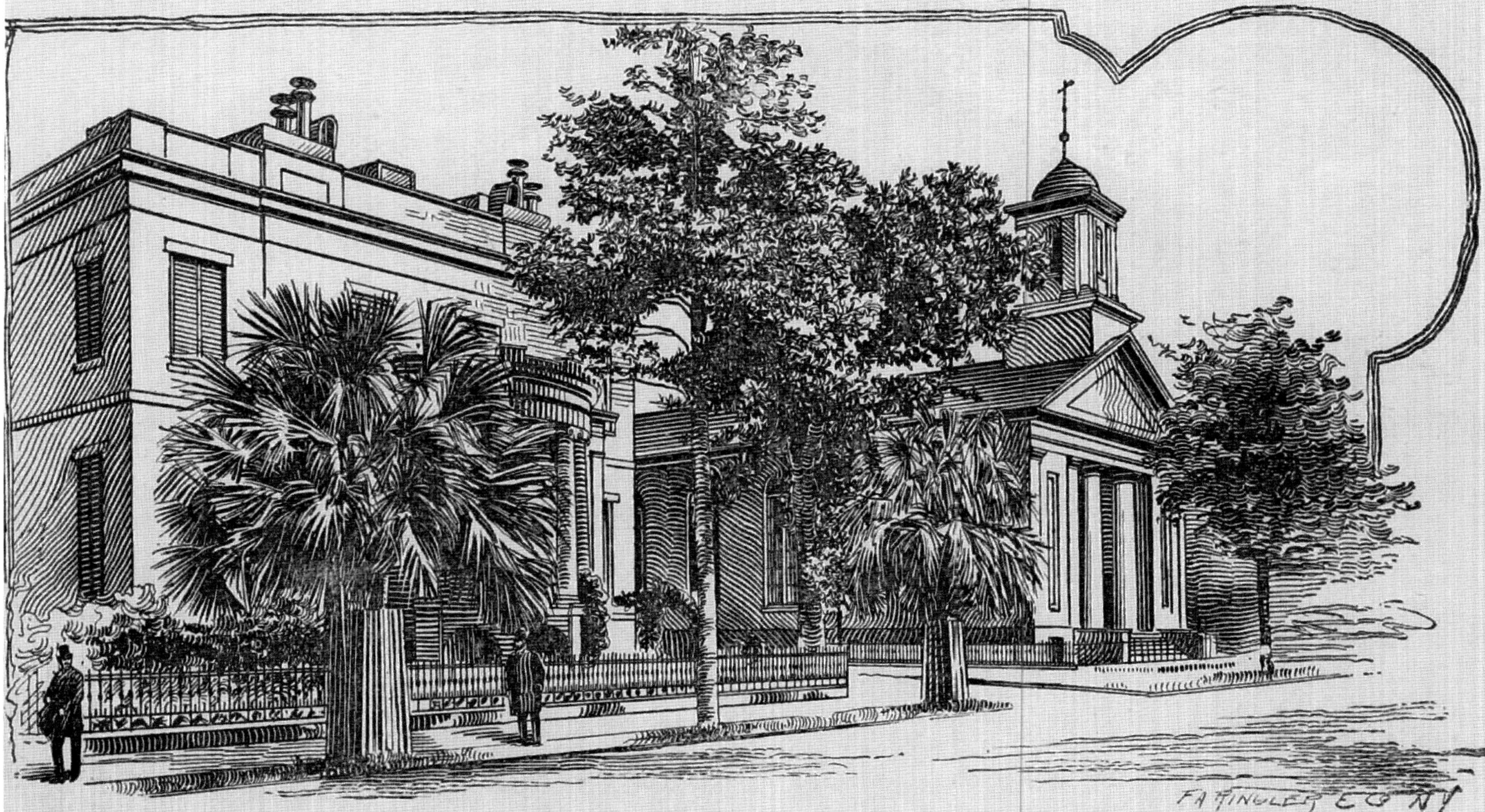

A BULL STREET RESIDENCE.

FIRST BAPTIST CHURCH.

SAVANNAH'S CHURCHES.

CHRIST CHURCH, on Bull street, fronting Johnson Square, is the mother church of the Episcopal Communion in Georgia. Christ Church parish was founded soon after the settlement of Savannah. The first edifice was begun in 1743, but was not completed until 1750. In 1796 it was destroyed by fire and was rebuilt upon an enlarged plan in 1803. The next year it was partly demolished by a hurricane and was not rebuilt until 1810. In 1838 the corner-stone of the present edifice was laid, the old church having been torn down, and the building was completed in 1840. The founder of Christ Church was Rev. Henry Herbert, who came over from England with Oglethorpe. John Wesley was its third rector, and on the site of the present edifice stood the rude chapel, in which he ministered as Chaplain to the colonists. The late Bishop Stephen Elliott was rector of the church from 1861 until his death, in 1866, and in the chancel is a beautiful window to his memory. The interior of the church is interesting. The chancel railing, table and stalls are handsomely carved, and the memorial lectern and font are works of art. The exterior presents a singular architectural appearance. Its style, partly Ionic, is rather financial than ecclesiastic, and the church is a solid and, not altogether, unimposing structure. It was in Christ Church that the first Sunday-school was established by John Wesley, nearly fifty years before Robert Raikes, who is honored as the founder of Sunday-schools, originated the scheme of Sunday instruction in Gloucester, England, and eighty years before the first Sunday-school in America, on the Raikes plan, was established.

ST. JOHN'S EPISCOPAL CHURCH, on Bull street, fronting Madison Square, is, architecturally, one of the finest churches in the city. It is on the English style of Gothic, with rich,

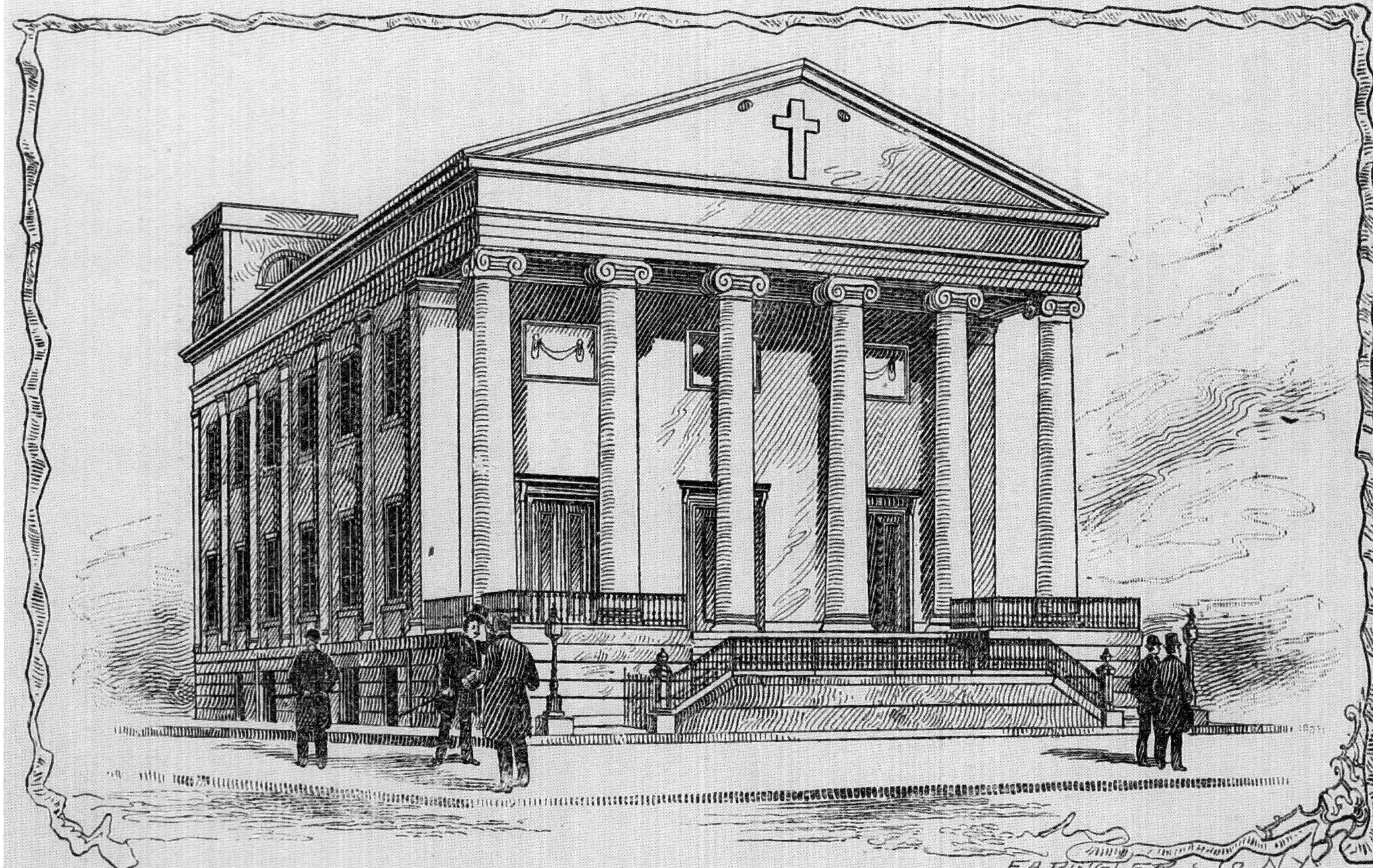

CHRIST CHURCH.

stained glass windows. The brass lectern, from which the design for the lectern in St. James Cathedral, Toronto, was taken, is an interesting work of art. The church was built in 1853. The parish was founded in 1841. Its first house of worship was on South Broad street, between Barnard and Jefferson. St. Matthews Episcopal Church, at Duffy and Barnard streets, is a mission of St. Johns.

THE EVANGELICAL LUTHERAN CHURCH OF THE ASCENSION, on Bull street, fronting Court-House Square, is the third edifice on the same site. The congregation was organized in 1750. The early records of the society are lost, but it is supposed to have been founded by two German preachers—Rubenhorst and Wottman. The present church was built in 1877.

THE INDEPENDENT PRESBYTERIAN CHURCH (rebuilding), at Bull and South Broad streets, will, when completed, be the finest church in the city, next to the Roman Catholic Cathedral. The first Presbyterian society in Savannah was organized in 1755 by Rev. John Zubly, D. D. The first church was on Market Square. It was destroyed in the fire of 1796 and another building was erected on Whitaker street, between President and York, where the Hanley building now stands. The steeple of the church was blown down and the building was partly demolished in the gale of 1804. It was repaired and used until 1819, when it was torn down and the congregation removed to the church at Bull and South Broad streets, which, up to its destruction in the fire of April, 1889, was one of the finest churches in the South. It is now being rebuilt upon exactly the same plan as the original church, and, when completed, will have cost $115,000. The burned edifice was begun in 1817 and was dedicated May 9, 1819. President James Monroe, who was visiting Savannah at the time, assisted, with his suite, in the ceremonies. The corner-stone for the present edifice was laid January 13, 1890.

THE FIRST PRESBYTERIAN CHURCH, on Bull street, fronting Monterey Square, is the second Presbyterian Church in

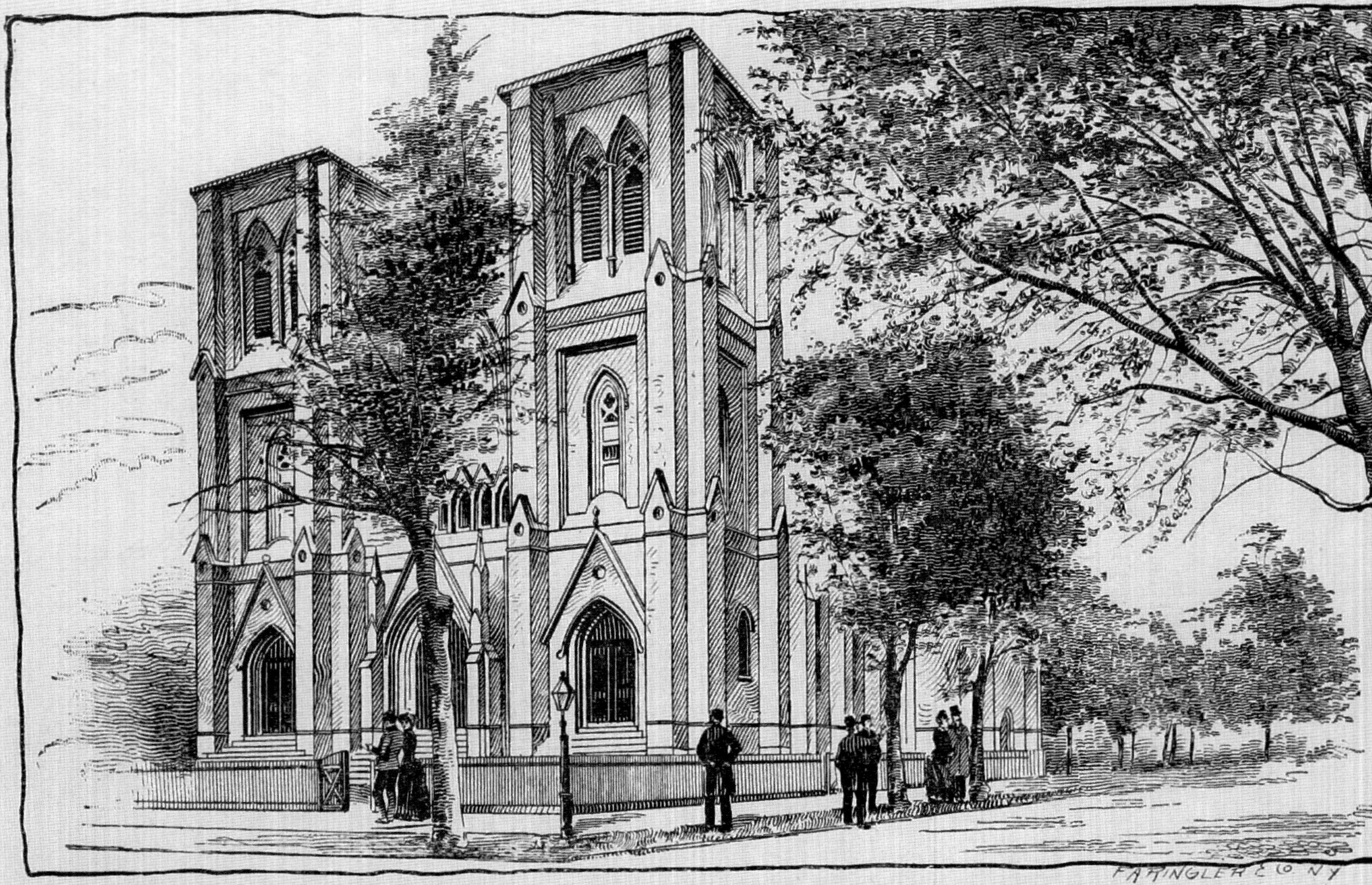

CATHEDRAL OF ST. JOHN THE BAPTIST.

Savannah. The congregation was organized in 1827. The first church was on Broughton street, between Barnard and Jefferson. The present edifice was begun in 1856, but it was not completed until after the war.

THE FIRST METHODIST PREACHER sent to Savannah was Brierly Allen, who arrived in Georgia in 1785. The first Methodist society was organized in 1806, and services were held at the houses of the members. The first church was begun in 1813 at the corner of Lincoln and South Broad streets, and was completed in 1816. It was called Wesley Chapel and still remains, but is occupied as residences.

WESLEY MONUMENTAL CHURCH, on Abercorn street, fronting Calhoun square, was begun in 1875 and was completed in 1889. The church, as its name indicates, is a monument to the great founder of Methodism.

TRINITY METHODIST CHURCH, or "Old Trinity," as it is sometimes called, because of its associations with the early history of Methodism in Savannah, is on Barnard street fronting Telfair place, and is the leading Methodist church in Savannah. The edifice is comparatively modern, having been built in 1848.

THE FIRST BAPTIST CHURCH, on Chippewa square, is the leading Baptist church in Savannah. It was built in 1833. The first Baptist society in Savannah was organized in 1795. A church was built in Franklin square, on the site of the present First African Baptist church, and was dedicated in 1800. It was occupied until the present church on Chippewa square was built thirty-three years later. The Duffy Street Baptist church is a mission of the First Baptist church.

THE ROMAN CATHOLIC RELIGION was established in Savannah during the latter part of the last century, after Georgia became a Royal Province. The first church was built in Liberty square, but was torn down in 1838. The Cathedral of St. John the Baptist, the *domus* of the Roman Catholic See of Savannah, on Abercorn street, fronting Lafayette square, is one of the finest ecclesiastical structures in the South. It originated with Bishop Ignatius Persico, now a

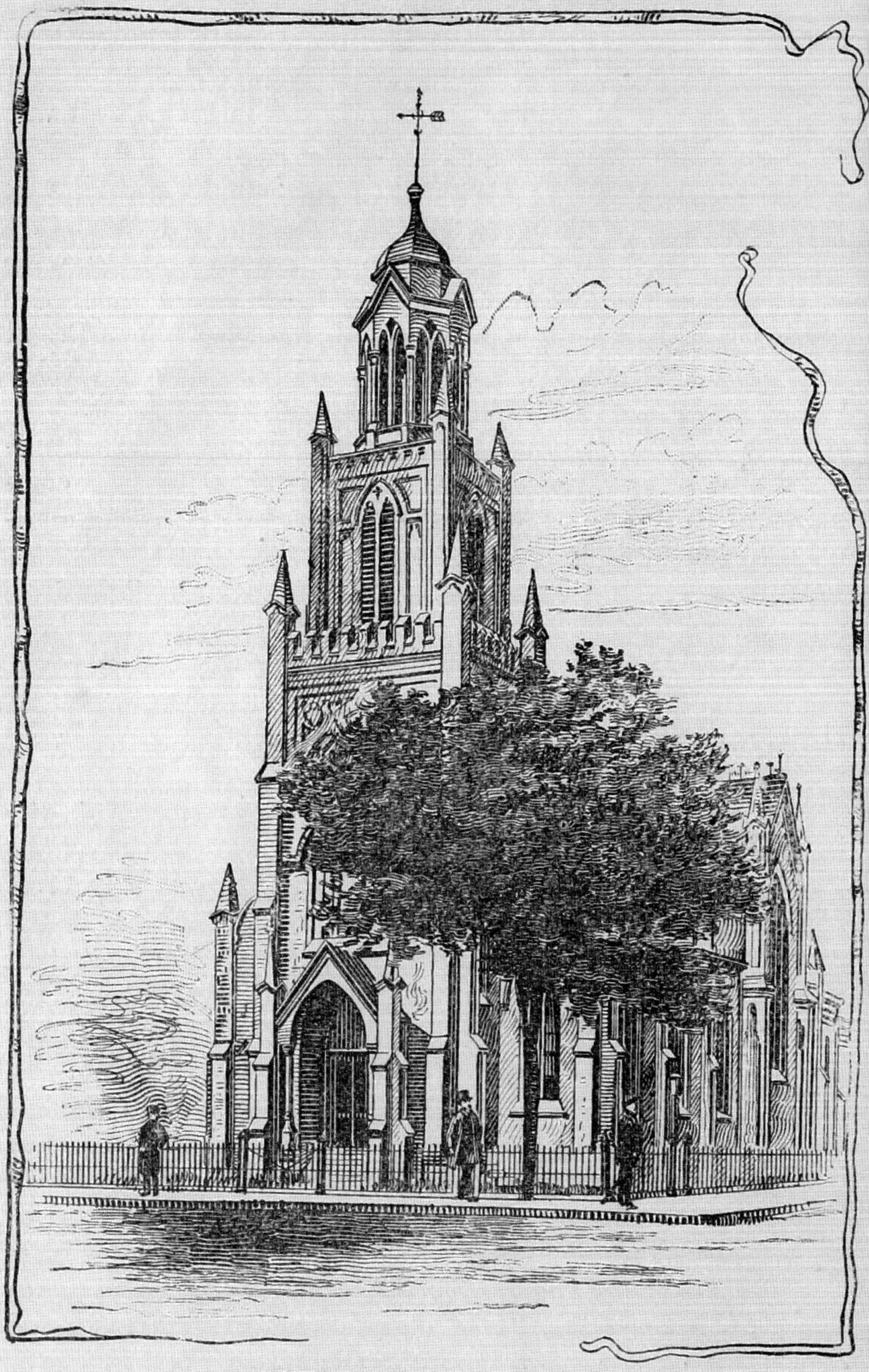

MICKVA ISRAEL SYNAGOGUE.

member of the papal household, who took the initial measures for its erection. The corner stone was laid in 1874 and the Cathedral was dedicated under the episcopacy of Bishop Gross, the present Archbishop of Oregon, in 1876. The architecture is French gothic, in the style of the great Notre Dame Cathedral of Paris, with nave and transepts. The interior is lofty and imposing; the triple rows of groined arches meeting at their apices, sixty-five feet above the floor, supported by columns of bronze exquisitely capped with original compositions. The sanctuary is fifty feet deep and its rail is ninety-nine feet in length. The main altar is of white marble. The principal side altars are to the Sacred Heart and to the Virgin and to St. Joseph. Above the altar to the Virgin is a copy of Murillo's "Immaculate Conception." Adjoining the Cathedral and connected with it by cloisters is the episcopal residence.

The Convent of St. Vincent de Paul is north of the Cathedral. The buildings consist of the convent cloisters and chapel and school rooms, covering the entire block fronting Liberty street between Abercorn and Lincoln streets. The convent was founded in 1842 by Rev. J. F. O'Neill, the pioneer priest of Georgia. It is the mother house of the Sisterhood of Mercy in the diocese. The convent possesses a number of interesting works of art. In the chapel is a representation in wood carving of the "Dead Christ" supported by the Virgin Mary. The work is a copy of the famous group executed for the Bishop of Minster in Westphalia. In the convent garden is a terra cotta statue of St. Benedict.

St. Patrick's Parish was founded in 1865. Its church at West Broad and Liberty streets is a handsome structure. Adjoining it is the pastor's house.

The first Hebrew congregation in Savannah was established by a colony of Israelites which came over shortly after Oglethorpe arrived. The congregation was called Mickva Israel. Its early history, however, is uncertain, as there are no records prior to its charter, which was granted in 1790. The corner stone of the present Mickva Israel Synagogue on Monterey square was laid in 1876, and the building was completed in 1878. The first synagogue was built in 1820 at the corner of Liberty and Whitaker streets. In 1829 it was destroyed by fire and a new edifice was built on the same site in 1841. The congregation B'Nai Brith Jacob has a synagogue at the corner of State and Montgomery streets, and the Chebrah Talmud Torah congregation worships in a house on Broughton street.

A SOCIETY OF SWEDENBORGIANS has existed in Savannah for many years, but until the Park New-Church, at Drayton and Huntingdon streets, fronting the park, was completed in 1889, the society was without a church edifice.

THE YOUNG MEN'S CHRISTIAN ASSOCIATION, at Bull and Jones streets, has a free reading room and amusement rooms, with evening classes and a gymnasium for the use of its members. The Association occupies its own building, which is open from 8 A. M. to 10 P. M.

THE COLORED CHURCHES of Savannah number about twenty. The Baptist and Methodist are the strongest denominations numerically. The colored Baptists have seven churches, one of which, the First African Baptist church in Franklin square, has over five thousand communicants. The Methodists have four churches, the Episcopalians two, Presbyterian and Congregational two, and Roman Catholic one.

ASYLUMS AND HOMES.

Savannah is rich in charitable and benevolent institutions. The oldest are the orphanage at Bethesda and the female Orphan Asylum at Bull and Charlton streets.

Bethesda is ten miles from Savannah by the public roads and eight miles by rail. The City and Suburban Railway runs regular trains to Bethesda station, and a walk of a third of a mile brings one to the historic place where Rev.

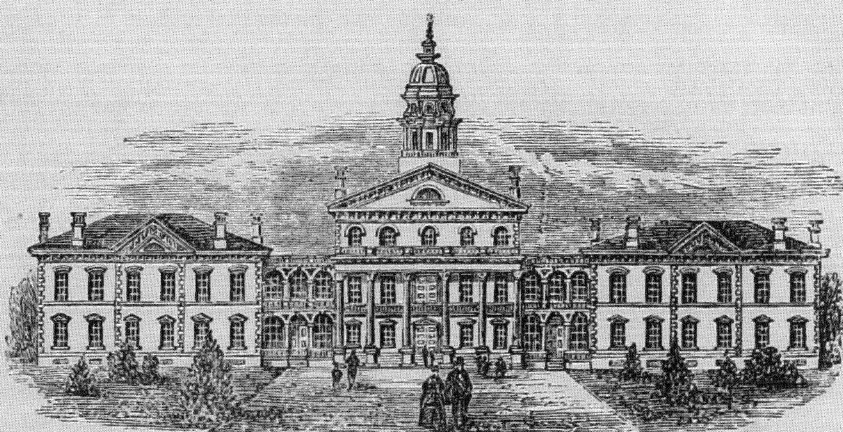

George Whitefield established his orphan house in 1740 The original buildings, towards the erection of which the people of two continents, aroused by the eloquent appeals of the great preacher for aid, gave with unbounded liberality, and the first bricks of which were laid by Whitefield's own hands, were struck by lightning and burned a short time after his death, which occurred in 1770. They were rebuilt, but were left in ruins when the British army evacuated the State. Lady Huntingdon, Whitefield's friend, labored with Christian zeal to forward the interests of Bethesda. At her death, which occurred in 1791, the school which she established was discontinued, and the State government, as successors to the trust, claimed the property. An unsuccessful attempt was made to establish Bethesda as a State institution, but in 1805 a fire damaged the Orphanage and a hurricane destroyed the outbuildings and the plantation. The Legislature ordered the property sold and the proceeds distributed among several charitable institutions, one of which was the Union Society. This society was founded in 1750, and its good works included the care of orphans and destitute children. Forty-five years after the sale and division of the Bethesda estate, the Union Society purchased one hundred and twenty-five acres of the property, which included the original site of Whitefield's Orphan House. Suitable buildings were erected, and the boys under the charge of the society were removed from Savannah to this historic spot. Bethesda was thus restored. During the civil war, owing to the proximity of the orphanage to the coast, the boys were removed and Confederate soldiers occupied the buildings. Upon the occupation of the country by the Federal army a detachment of Federal soldiers was stationed at Bethesda. Shortly after the close of the war the orphan house was re-established. In 1870 the main building of the present orphanage was built, and ten years later the western wing was added. The eastern wing is still unbuilt. Through the liberality of one of its members the society was enabled to build and equip a technological department. There are one hundred boys now under the charge of the society. All have the benefits of the school, and the larger boys are instructed in the mechanical arts. In addition to these instructions they are required to assist in farm work. The discipline is positive but gentle, conforming more to that of a family than to that of a semi-public institution. The boys, although bound to the society until they arrive at the age of eighteen, are allowed to leave at any time, provided there are satisfactory reasons for their doing so. The orphan house is supported by a small income obtained from rentals of city property and the yearly dues of the members of the society. Bethesda is open at all times to visitors. The President of the society is Colonel J. H. Estill, who has had charge of the interests of the Bethesda

Orphanage longer than any person except its founder, George Whitefield.

The Female Orphan Asylum had a common origin with the Union Society in 1750, for the care and education of orphan and destitute children in general, who enjoyed its charities, without distinction of sex, until December 17, 1801, when the sexes were separated. The Female Orphan Asylum began then a distinct existence, the boys remaining with the Union Society. It is one of the many venerable institutions of which the city boasts.

The Abrams Widows' Home, at East Broad and Broughton streets, was founded through the generosity of a noble-hearted Christian woman of that name. As its name suggests, it is a home for indigent widows. Unsectarian in its character its benefits are enjoyed by all sects, and its kindly charities are poured out without reference to the distinctions of society.

The Episcopal Orphans' Home, at Liberty and Jefferson streets, was founded in 1854. It is under the patronage of the Episcopal church. The present asylum building was erected in 1886.

The Industrial Relief Society and the Home for the Friendless, at Drayton and Charlton streets, was incorporated in 1849, and was organized in 1875. It is a refuge for indigent women.

St. Mary's Orphans' Home, at Habersham and St. Paul streets, is a Roman Catholic institution for the care of orphan girls, and is under the patronage of the Female Orphan Benevolent Society.

The Little Minnie Mission, a home for waifs, at Jones and Lincoln streets, was established through the charity of Mrs. Charles M. Green.

The Widow's Home, at West Broad and President streets, was founded by Miss Mary Telfair.

The Asylum of the Little Sisters of the Poor, at Drayton and Perry streets, established in 1890, is the first institu-

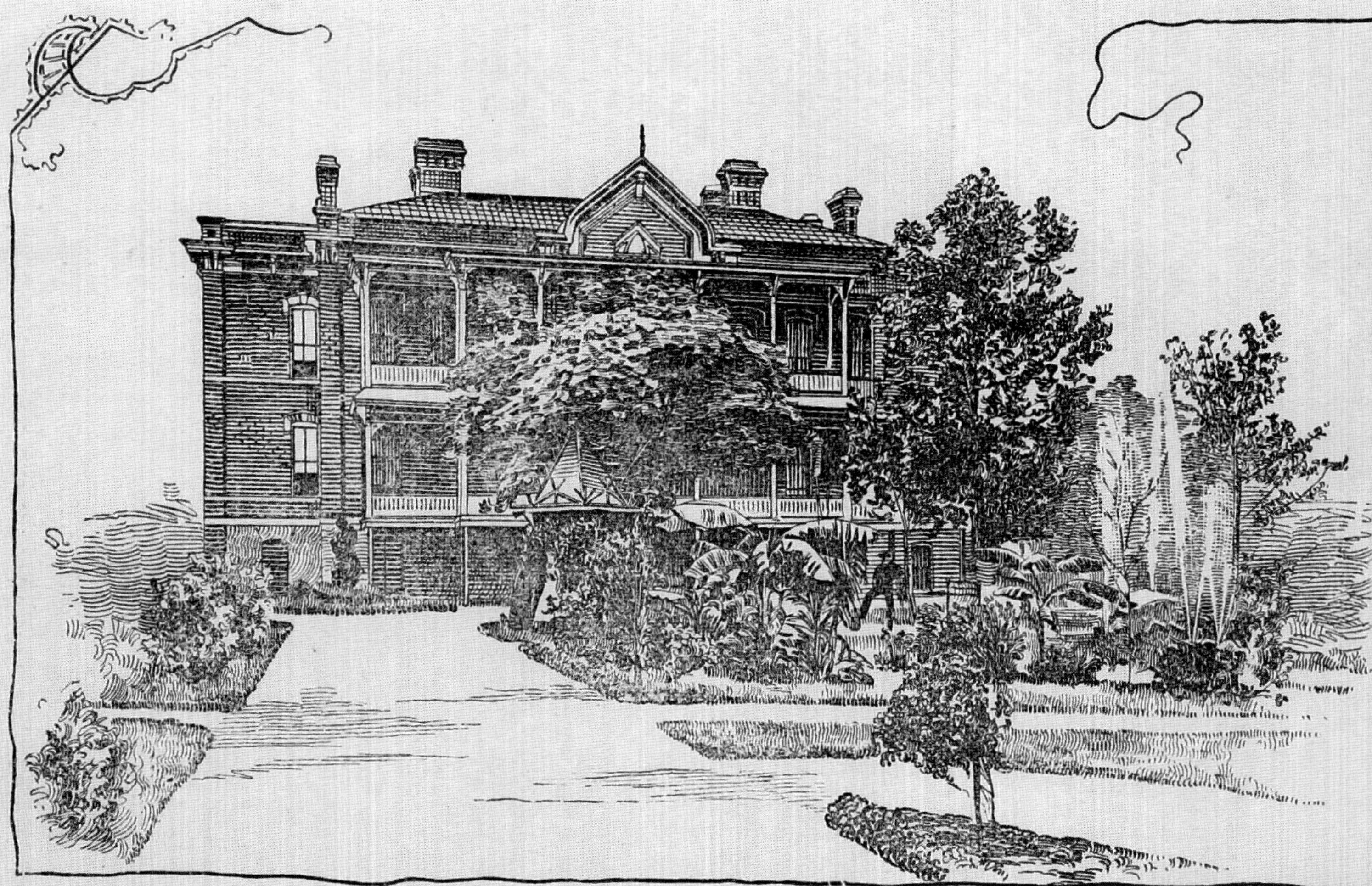

TELFAIR HOSPITAL AND GROUNDS.

tion of the Sisterhood in the South. It is under the patronage of the Roman Catholic church.

THE SACRED HEART ORPHANAGE, for colored children, on St. James street, is under the patronage of the Roman Catholic church.

THE HOSPITALS.

THE SAVANNAH HOSPITAL, at Huntingdon and Drayton streets, was incorporated in 1835. It is not a municipal charity, but a private corporation. It receives from the city, however, an annual appropriation for the treatment of the poor. The hospital building and grounds are among the finest in the South. The visiting days are Wednesdays and Sundays from 2 to 6 o'clock P. M.

ST. JOSEPH'S INFIRMARY, at the corner of Taylor and Habersham streets, is the hospital of the Sisters of Mercy. It was organized in June, 1875, and is supported by voluntary contributions and pay patients. Its charities are extended without distinction of creed. Visitors are received at any time.

THE TELFAIR HOSPITAL FOR FEMALES, at New Houston and Drayton streets, was founded in 1883 through a bequest by Miss Mary Telfair. It is one of the best arranged hospitals in the South. The visiting days are Tuesdays and Fridays from 3 to 6 o'clock P. M.

THE GEORGIA INFIRMARY for colored people on Sixth street, is supported by an appropriation by the city and by contributions.

CEMETERIES.

LAUREL GROVE is the principal burial place of Savannah. It is nearest to the city of any of the suburban cemeteries, and although not as famous for its scenery as Bonaventure, it is one of the most interesting places around Savannah. It is within fifteen minutes ride by horse car of the hotels. The cemetery was established in 1852, and the first interment was in October of that year. It is situated on high ground surrounded by native forests and is a picturesque and beautiful spot. Its establishment was rendered necessary by the crowded condition of the old cemetery on South Broad street, which has been a burial place for more than a century. The Confederate soldiers' lot in Laurel Grove is one of the most interesting spots in the cemetery. Here repose nearly fifteen hundred heroes of the civil war, whose remains were gathered from the distant battlefields on which they fell and were given a soldier's burial. The noble work was accomplished by the Ladies' Memorial Association of Savannah, which, with sacred care, has watched over their graves, and on Memorial Day decorates them with the bright flowers of spring. A marble statute of "Silence," which was originally one of the statues of the Confederate monument in the parade ground, keeps guard over this "bivouac of the heroic dead." Each grave is marked by a neat marble headstone.

THE JEWISH CEMETERY is a part of Laurel Grove. The Jews' old burying grounds are on the western limits of the city, and are small enclosures shut in by high brick walls. One of them, the ruins of which only remain, was a burying ground before the Revolution, and within its walls was the rallying place of the American and French forces after their repulse at the battle of Spring Hill in 1779. The other

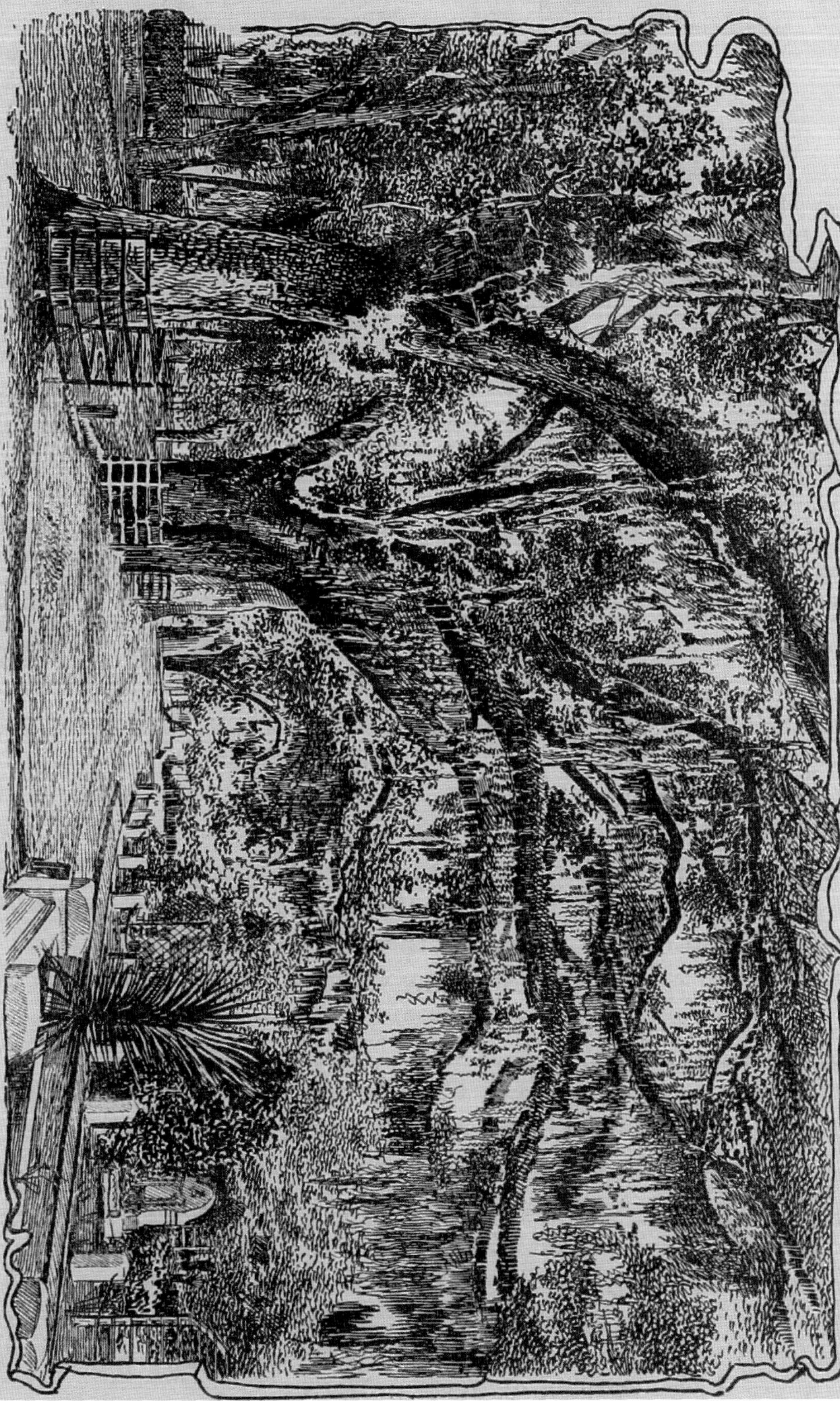

burying ground is a few yards south. Neither has been used for many years.

THE COLORED BURYING GROUND is a part of Laurel Grove, and is just beyond the main enclosure. To a stranger it is worth a visit.

THE CATHEDRAL CEMETERY, the Roman Catholic burial place, is on the Thunderbolt shell road and the Coast Line railroad, two miles from the city. The cemetery was founded in 1852, and contains forty-five acres. It is handsomely laid off and contains many fine mounds. It is the burial place of Bishops Barry, Baron and Gartland. Before the Cathedral cemetery was founded the Roman Catholic burial place was a part of the old cemetery on South Broad street.

THE OLD BURYING GROUND on South Broad street is one of the oldest cemeteries in America. It was closed in 1852. The ancient vaults and tombs still remain, although they are rapidly crumbling away. The history of the cemetery is obscure. It was originally the burial place for Christ church parish. Up to 1763 it contained about half an acre of ground, but in that year it was enlarged. Savannah had been settled thirty-one years before it required an acre of ground in which to bury its dead. In 1768 the cemetery was made a public burial place. It is surrounded by a high brick wall and the interior is grown up with weeds and briers. It contains the tombs of many of the early colonists of Georgia. The oldest graves, in what was the original burying ground, are midway between the South Broad street gate and the Abercorn street gate. The inscriptions on many of the old slabs are so worn away that they are scarcely legible. The graves of three of Christ church's early rectors—Bartholomew Zouberbuhler, died September 2, 1766, rector of the parish twenty-one years; Samuel Frink, died October 4, 1771; Edward Ellington, died 1795—are marked with broad stone slabs and are objects of interest. General Nathaniel Greene was buried here, and the cemetery contains the graves of many heroes of the Revolution whose names are familiar to history. Sir Patrick Houston, baronet, president of His

Majesty's Council of Georgia, who died in 1762, and Lady Houston, who died in 1775, are also buried here.

EVERGREEN CEMETERY (Bonaventure) is four miles from the city on the Thunderbolt shell road and the Coast Line railroad, on the banks of the Thunderbolt River. Its natural beauty, with its historic associations, render it one of the most interesting places near Savannah. It contains one hundred and forty acres, seventy of which are enclosed. The cemetery was established in 1869.

THE MILITARY.

Savannah is pre-eminently a military city. Nowhere in the South is the military *esprit du corps* maintained with such ardor and enthusiasm. The chivalric spirit has always been high. The earliest picture of Savannah represents a few scattered houses surrounded by a wall of forest with a battery of cannon commanding the river. The colony was planted upon ground claimed by the Spaniards, and within easy reach of the strong fortress of St. Augustine, from which the land and naval forces of Philip V were hurled against the little handful of Englishmen. A regiment was one of the first of Oglethorpe's necessities, and from the beginning the colonists felt that the safety of their altars and firesides depended upon stout arms and brave hearts. The spirit then born has never since died. The soldiery which Savannah sent to four wars has illustrated the prowess of Southern chivalry. During the civil war Savannah furnished over three thousand troops to the confederate service. Its leading military organizations—the First Volunteer Regiment of Georgia, the Chatham Artillery, Savannah Volunteer Guards and the Georgia Hussars—antedate the civil war by more than half a century.

THE CHATHAM ARTILLERY, the oldest artillery company but one in the United States, was organized May 1, 1786, its birth being coeval with the termination of the Revolution. The company bears to Savannah the same relation that the Ancient and Honorable Artillery of Massachusetts does to Boston. A month after its organization it discharged its first mournful duty at the funeral of General Nathaniel Greene, and it fired minute guns at Washington's funeral. During the war of 1812 it formed a part of the garrison of Fort Jackson. When the corner stones of the Pulaski and Greene monuments were laid in 1825 it participated in the ceremony and fired a salute in honor of Lafayette. During the civil war it served at Fort Pulaski and other points around Savannah, and took a conspicuous part in the battles of Olustee and Battery Wagner, and served with the western army until its surrender. Its connection with the military service of the Confederacy began with the occupation of Fort Pulaski in 1861 and continued until the last gun of the war had been fired. The company took part in the Yorktown centennial in 1876, and celebrated its own centennial in 1886. It is an interesting fact that during the civil war the Chatham Artillery furnished from its membership to the confederate and state service more than fifty commissioned officers.

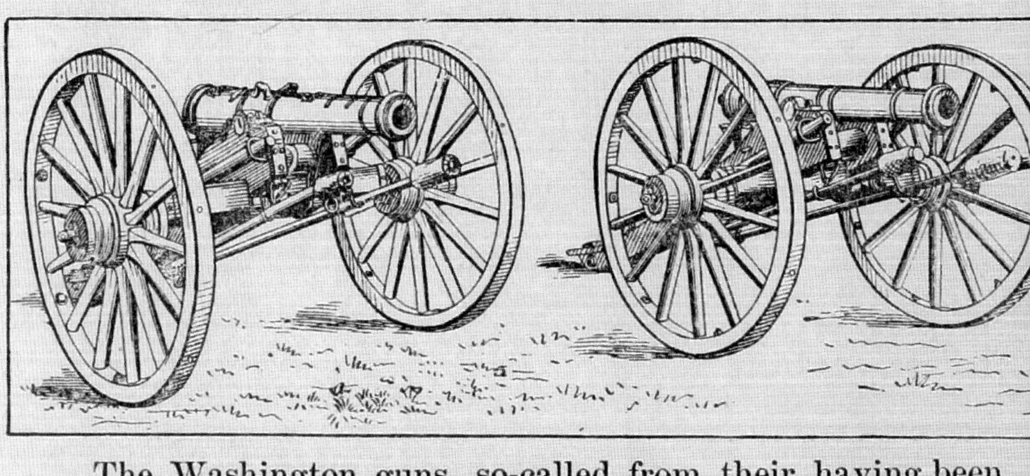

The Washington guns, so-called from their having been presented to the Chatham Artillery by General Washington, shortly after his visit to Savannah in 1791, are relics around which cluster the memories of many historic events. They were used against the Continental army during the Revolution, and were surrendered by Lord Cornwallis at Yorktown. Their possession by the Chatham Artillery has always been guarded with jealous devotion. When the Confederate army evacuated Savannah, to prevent their falling into the hands of the enemy they were buried under the armory. Many efforts were made by the Union soldiers to find them. The armory yard and beneath the basement were even probed with iron rods. So securely were the guns hidden that after the war they were with great difficulty recovered.

THE GEORGIA HUSSARS, which were a part of the famous "Jeff Davis Legion" during the civil war, were organized shortly after the war of 1812, by the consolidation of the Chatham Hussars and the Chatham Light Dragoons, the latter of which was an organized command as early as 1781, and officiated with the Chatham Artillery at the funeral of General Greene in 1786. The troop was constantly on duty with the Chatham Artillery, the Savannah Volunteer Guards, the Republican Blues and other companies of which no record is in existence, during the war of 1812. The Hussars are now a part of the First Georgia Regiment of Cavalry.

THE SAVANNAH VOLUNTEER GUARDS is the oldest infantry corps in Georgia. In consequence of the loss of its early records and the inaccessibility of other sources of accurate information, if such are still in existence, the history of the corps prior to 1818 is obscure. It was organized in 1802, and one of its first parades was during the visit of Vice-President Aaron Burr to Savannah. It was on duty during the war of 1812, and a part of the corps was sent to Florida on an expedition againt St. Augustine. Later on in 1819 it took part in the reception of President Monroe and in 1825 it paraded in honor of Lafayette. It took a conspicuous part in the civil war, and surrendered with Lee at Appomattox. It is now composed of three companies. Its temporary armory is on Madison square.

THE FIRST VOLUNTEER REGIMENT OF GEORGIA, whose history as a part of the militia organization goes back to the Revolutionary war, is composed of five companies—the Republican Blues, organized in 1808, the Irish Jasper Greens in 1843, the German Volunteers in 1846, the Oglethorpe Light Infantry in 1856 and the Savannah Cadets in 1861. The regimental armory is at Abercorn and Huntingdon streets.

THE COLORED MILITARY, also a part of the state forces, numbers about five hundred men, and is composed of the First Georgia Battalion of six companies, organized in 1878, the Georgia Artillery and the Savannah Hussars.

THE OLD FORTIFICATIONS.

The defenses of Savannah during the civil war still remain, except where they have been leveled to make room for the city's growth. Four lines of defense were adopted, but only three were built. The first, or exterior line, was built early in the war to protect the coast from attacks by the Federal navy and to prevent the landing of troops. It extended from Causton's Bluff, four miles east of Savannah, to the Ogeechee River, and embraced Greenwich Park, Thunderbolt, Isle of Hope and Beaulieu. Detached works were built on Whitmarsh, Oatland, Skidaway and Green Islands, but these were only occupied a portion of the time, and towards the close of the war were abandoned. The general character of the works was water batteries, constructed of earth, and reveted with sand bags, sods and fascines, and with traverses.

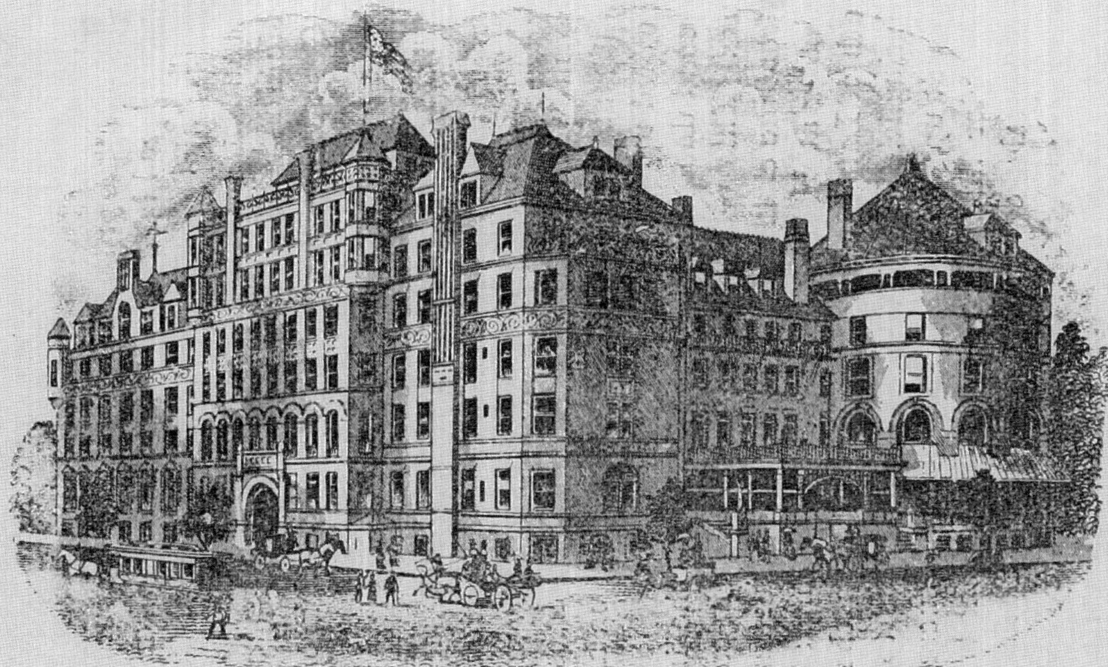

THE DE SOTO HOTEL.

The river batteries at and around Fort Jackson were intended for the protection of the main water approach. Fort Bartow, through which the Tybee railroad now runs, was the most important of these works and was the largest and most complete fortification on the coast. It was a bastioned work enclosing an area of seventeen acres, with glacis, moat, curtains, bomb proofs and surgeons' rooms under ground, and with advanced batteries and rifle pits in front, near the water. The ruins of the fortification, although overgrown with trees and bushes, are worth visiting.

Fort McAllister, on the south bank of the Ogeechee River at Genesis Point, was an enclosed work of about an acre, detached and isolated, irregular in form, but compactly built, and adapted to its condition and surroundings. The armament was heavy, and the gallant and successful defenses it repeatedly made against the Federal iron clads, and Sherman's corps from the land side, have given it a name and place in the history of Savannah's defenses. Though an insignificant earth work, it was, by location and circumstances, called upon to act a giant's part.

The second line was what was known as the interior line of defense. This was almost semi-circular in contour, and distant from the city an average of three-fourths of a mile; its left resting at Fort Boggs; its right resting at a point a little south of Laurel Grove cemetery, and on the low lands of the Springfield plantation. The line was to resist any direct assault upon the city, should a force succeed in passing the exterior line. It consisted of detached lunettes at regular intervals, constructed with mutual flank defense, and having sectors of fire, covering the entire space in front of the line, all growth having been cut for half a mile in advance. The curtains were not of the same heavy character as the lunettes, but consisted of rifle pits and covered ways for direct communication. Abattis were constructed in front of the many lunettes. No portion of this line was ever subjected to attack.

Fort Boggs, on the left of the line, was a bastioned work about an acre and a half in area. Fort Brown, near the Catholic cemetery, was a point of some importance, more, however, from its early location and construction than any special merit. The earthwork crosses the Thunderbolt shell road just beyond the cemetery and the fort is near by.

It was not until the early part of 1864, when Sherman's army was gradually approaching the coast, that it was thought necessary to fortify Savannah inland. At this juncture a line of defense was adopted and constructed on the west of Savannah. The right of the line rested on the Savannah River, four miles from the city; the left rested on Salt Creek, about seven miles from the city. The defense consisted of detached works, continuously connected with rifle pits. The natural defense was very great; the swamps and low lands on the front of the line in many places being impenetrable and making it difficult of approach. This was the line upon which the defense of Savannah was made for eight days and maintained successfully against Sherman's forces, and which a picket's guard held while the city was evacuated.

In the war of 1812 the city's line of defense extended from the foot of Broughton street to the west side of Lafayette square, and crossed the site of the present Cathedral of St. John the Baptist. It then diverged and followed the present line of Liberty street lane across Bull street, where the De Soto now stands, to Spring Hill, occupied by the Central railroad passenger depot, and thence to the foot of Farm street. The ruins of these defenses have long since disappeared.

FORT PULASKI.

Fort Pulaski is the principal object of interest at the entrance to the harbor. It is on Cockspur Island, fourteen miles from the city, and commands both entrances to the river. It was named after Count Pulaski. Its siege and capture are a memorable event in the history of the civil

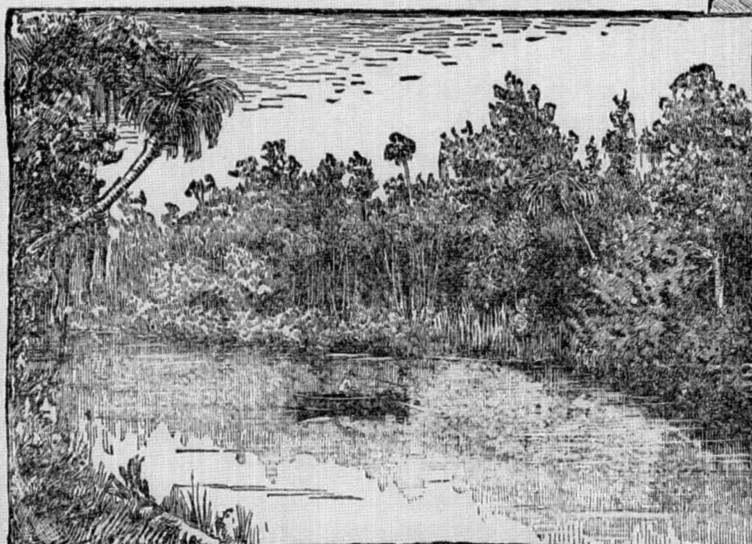

SCENE ON SAVANNAH RIVER.

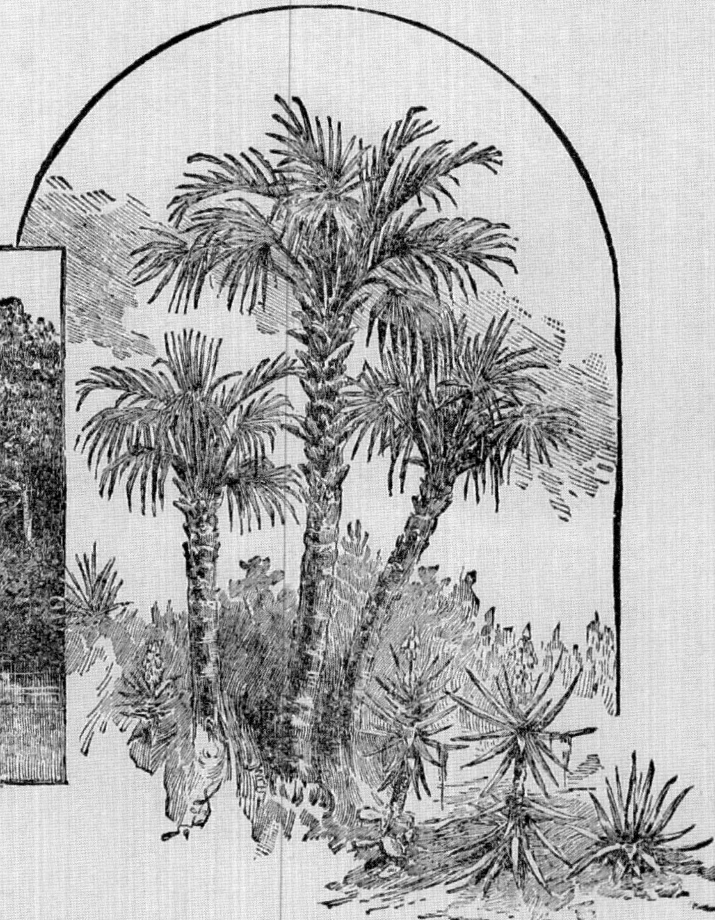

PALMETTO AND SPANISH BAYONET.

war. The fort was begun in 1831, and was sixteen years in building and cost over a million of dollars. Its walls contain over thirteen millions of brick. It has five faces and is casemated on all sides. The walls are seven and a half feet thick and rise twenty-five feet above the water. The fort was built for an armament of one hundred and forty guns. The gorge is covered with an earthwork of bold relief. The main work and the demilune are both surrounded and divided by a wide ditch.

The fort was taken possession of by Georgia troops early in 1861, and was occupied until after the capture of Tybee Island and the advance of the Federal batteries. Its bombardment April 10, 1862, was from King's Landing on Tybee Island, three-quarters of a mile distant. Early on the morning of the bombardment Major General Hunter, of the Federal army, dispatched an officer in an open boat, bearing a flag of truce, with a summons to the commanding officer in the fort to surrender. To this Colonel Charles H. Olmstead, the commandant, laconically and heroically replied: "I am here to defend the fort, not to surrender it." Upon the receipt of this reply by the Federal commander, orders were issued for the commencement of the bombardment, which lasted for twenty-seven hours. The second day at noon all but two of the casemate guns bearing on Tybee were dismounted, and but two of the barbette guns were left; the outer walls of two of the casemates had been shot away, and others were in a crumbling condition; the moat was bridged over by the ruins of the walls; most of the traverses were riddled; the officers' quarters were damaged; the magazine was in momentary danger of being exploded, and all avenues of escape for the garrison being cut off, a surrender was determined upon and the fort capitulated. After the Federal forces took possession, the damages to the casemates were repaired. The garrison was withdrawn shortly after the close of hostilities and only a sergeant was left in charge. The fort is in full view of steamers entering the harbor and is an object of interest to strangers. It is reached only by special boats, which land through permission from the United States army engineers' office in Savannah.

Three miles below the city on the south bank of the river is Fort Oglethorpe, formerly known as Fort Jackson, after Governor James Jackson. It was originally a small brick work projected in 1808, and occupied during the war of 1812–15, since which time it has been rebuilt, and is now an important element in the river defense of Savannah.

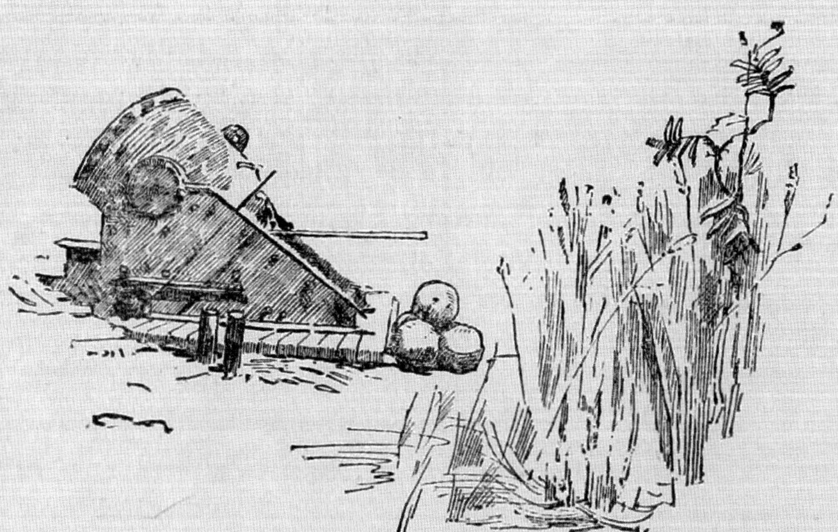

SAVANNAH'S RESORTS.

SAVANNAH abounds in beautiful resorts, famous for their situation, scenery and historic interest. Thunderbolt, Warsaw beach, Greenwich Park, Bonaventure, Isle of Hope, Montgomery, Beaulieu, White Bluff and Tybee beach are the principal resorts, each with its own attraction. The country around Savannah is attractive for its peculiarities of landscape. The scenery is characteristic in its beauty. The principal drives are over the Thunderbolt and White Bluff shell roads, magnificent roadways, lined with majestic oaks and towering pines and rich farms of unlimited fertility. A visit to Savannah without a drive over its shell roads is incomplete. In midwinter wild roses and jasmine bloom among the hedges, mingled with the hanging moss, and magnolias and the tall sycamore form avenues of beauty nowhere else to be found.

An afternoon drive under the stately oaks of Bonaventure, with a view of the great salt marshes, and along the river bluff to Greenwich Park, and back to the city in twilight, is one of the most charming features of a day's sightseeing. At sunset Bonaventure presents a scene unequaled in picturesqueness. The wide solemn avenues, with here and there a marble shaft penetrating the shadows, the phantom-like arms of the dark broad-spreading oaks with their motionless pendants of pale gray moss, form a picture of weird and wonderful beauty.

The country east of Savannah to the Thunderbolt river is

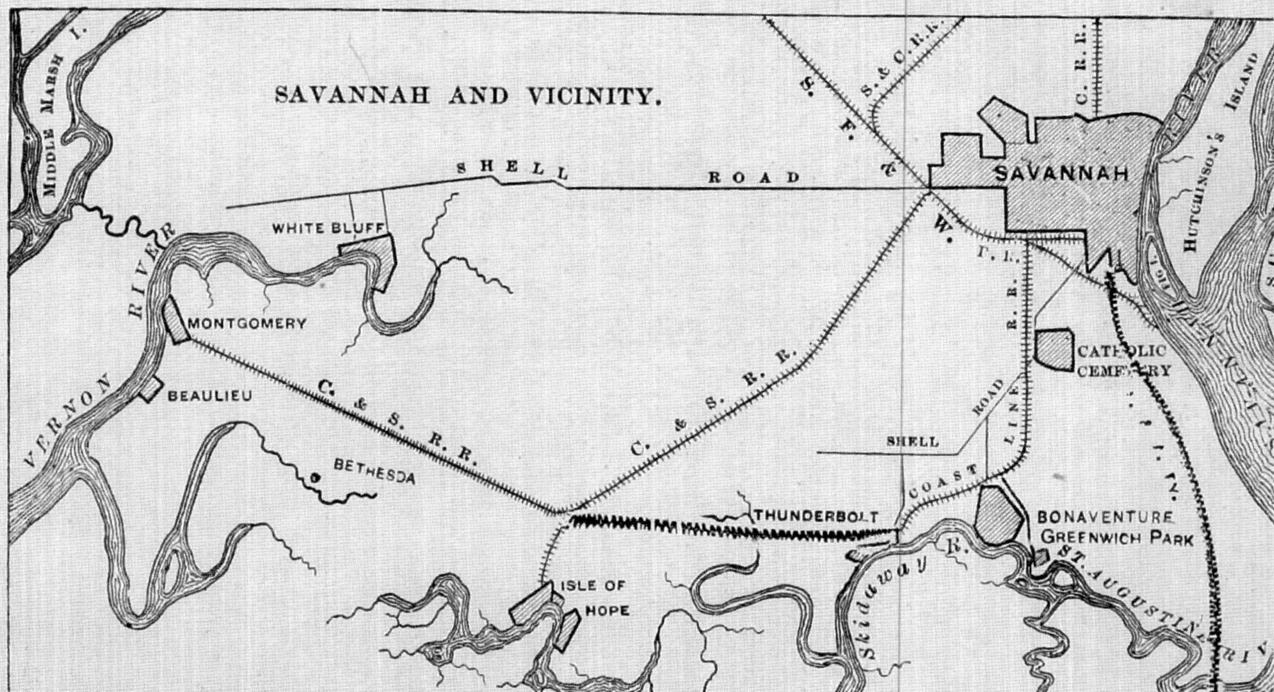

SAVANNAH AND VICINITY.
SAVANNAH
SHELL ROAD
S. F. & W.
S. & C. R. R.
C. R. R.
C. & S. R. R.
C. & S. R. R.
COAST LINE R. R.
SHELL ROAD
MIDDLE MARSH I.
VERNON RIVER
WHITE BLUFF
MONTGOMERY
BEAULIEU
BETHESDA
THUNDERBOLT
ISLE OF HOPE
Skidaway R.
BONAVENTURE
GREENWICH PARK
ST. AUGUSTINE RIV.
HUTCHINSON'S ISLAND
RIVER
S. C.

occupied by farms; beyond is a great expanse of salt marshes between the main land and the sea islands. To the north is Hutchinson's Island, between the Savannah River and Back River. The island formerly belonged to South Carolina, but was purchased by the city several years ago, and a part of it is occupied by rice plantations. West of the city are rich farms and to the south are thousands of acres of fertile land. The principal rice plantations are along the Savannah and Back Rivers, above and below the city, and on the Ogeechee River some some distance south of Savannah. Savannah's resorts on the salts are beyond the immediate suburbs with farms intervening. The seaside resorts are within easy reach by rail or boat.

BONAVENTURE.

Bonaventure has long been famous among the places of interest around Savannah, for its natural beauty and its historic and romantic associations. There are many fine monuments in the cemetery, but no marble can vie in beauty and grandeur with the mighty yet graceful oaks which spread their arched boughs and superb foliage over the wide avenues. The cemetery is reached by a drive of four miles over the Thunderbolt shell road, or by the Coast Line railroad. It derives its name from the original tract of land of which it formed a part. The corporate name of the cemetery is Evergreen.

The place was first settled about 1760 by Colonel John Mulryne, who came to this country from England and removed from South Carolina to Georgia. By marriage the property passed into the possession of the Tattnall family, and it was here that Governor Tattnall was born in 1765. The first house built by Colonel Mulryne was upon the high ground overlooking Thunderbolt River and facing the center walk of the old garden which extended in terraces from the plateau to the river. This house was destroyed by fire in the latter part of the last century, during a dinner entertainment. The roof taking fire first, all hope of saving the building was abandoned and the dinner was removed to the trees and there finished. The marriage of Colonel Mulryne's daughter, Mary, and Josiah Tattnall is of peculiar interest in the history of Bonaventure, since from it date the avenues of magnificent trees which form the pride and chief feature of interest of the place. The trees were planted about that time, and tradition has it, in the forms of the letters M and T, the initials of the Mulryne and Tattnall families. A second house, built by Governor Tattnall, was also destroyed by fire. This house stood in the open space in the rear of the site occupied by the first, and its location is marked by a large cedar tree, nourished by the ashes of the burnt hearth.

In 1847 the property passed into the hands of Captain P. Wiltberger, who had long associated the quiet and peace of the place, its patriarch trees, and their deep, solemn shade, its calm and seclusion, with a cemetery. With him originated the idea of devoting Bonaventure to its present and final use, and his remains sleep under the foliage of its trees. Circumstances prevented for a time the execution of Capt. Wiltberger's plans, but they were taken up by his son, Major W. H. Wiltberger, and the formation of the Evergreen Cemetery Company, in 1869, was the result of his efforts The first person buried at Bonaventure was the wife of Governor Tattnall, who died there in 1803, and who was shortly afterward followed to the grave by her honored husband. Amongst the historical incidents of the place is the rescue of Governor Wright, by Colonel Mulryne, during the revolutionary war. Colonel Mulryne, a staunch tory, disapproved of the Declaration of Independence, and when the patriots confined Governor Wright in Savannah, Mulryne hastened to his rescue, and conveyed him to Bonaventure until he could be placed on board an English man-of-war lying in the river. Colonel Mulryne left the country with the Governor, and died at Nassau, New Providence. It is also historic that the French, after their unsuccessful attack on Savannah, fell back to Bonaventure and thence re-embarked many of their wounded, burying a number of their dead on the place.

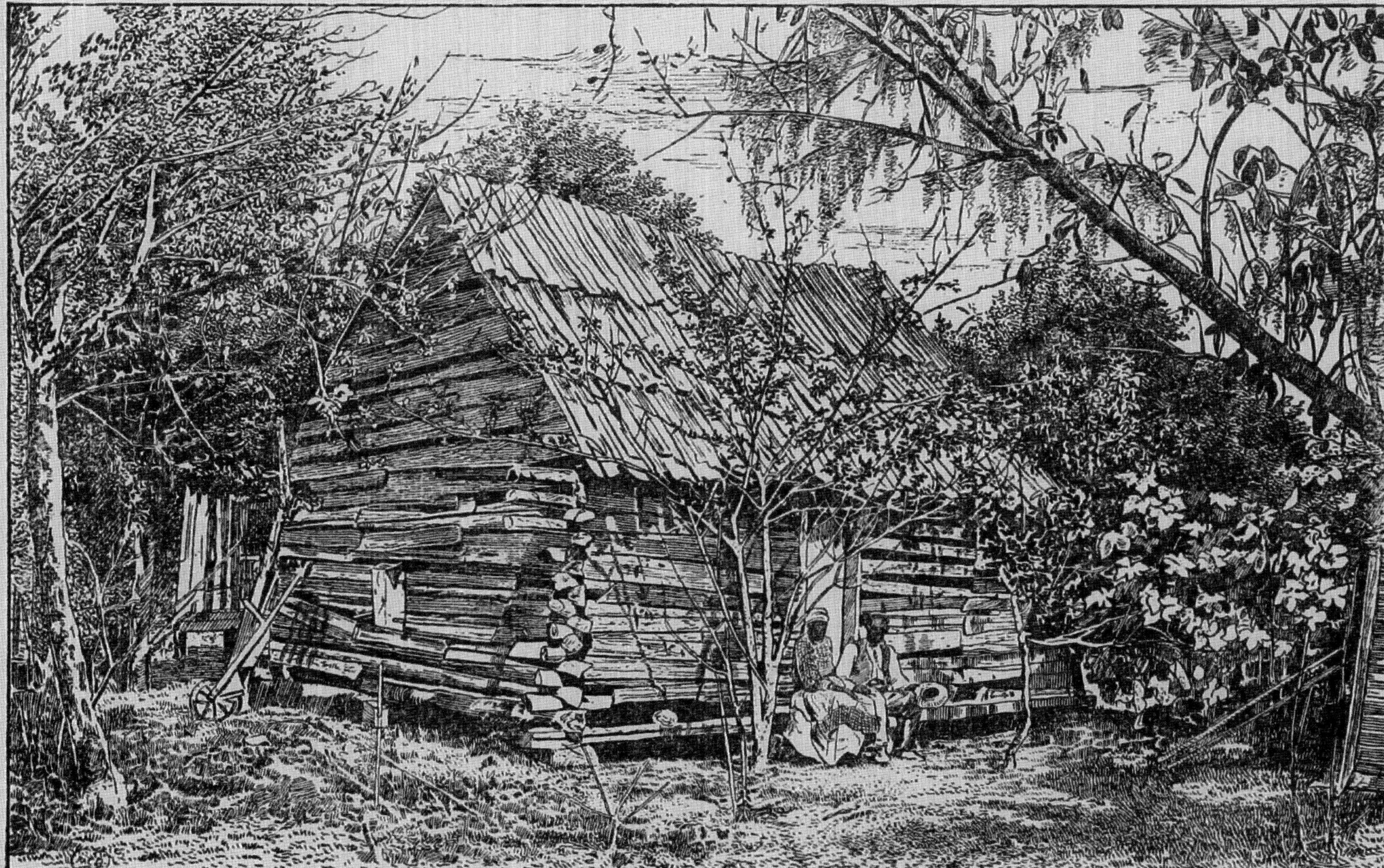

CABIN ON GREEN ISLAND.

THUNDERBOLT.

Thunderbolt, on Thunderbolt River, four miles from Savannah, is one of its most popular resorts. It is the terminus of the Coast Line railroad and of the Thunderbolt shell road. There is nothing peculiarly striking about the place, other than its invigorating sea breezes, fine oaks, delightful shade, good salt bathing and excellent fish and oysters. It is the main source of the fish and oyster supply for the Savannah market. It is the headquarters of the Savannah Yacht Club, whose handsome club house and grounds occupy a charming site on the bluff just north of the village, in full view of Greenwich Park and Bonaventure and commanding a magnificent view of the river and the marshes, and of the sea islands. All of the regattas under the auspices of the Savannah Yacht Club are sailed over the Thunderbolt course. The Thunderbolt race track is just west of the village. According to local tradition, the place received its name from the fall of a thunderbolt and the gushing forth of a spring from the spot where the bolt struck. Whether the tradition be founded on fact or not, it is nevertheless believed to be true, and the spring is pointed out with faith and pride by old inhabitants as the Thunderbolt spring.

Warsaw beach is reached in the summer by steamers from Thunderbolt. It is a magnificent bathing ground and is a popular resort.

GREENWICH PARK.

Greenwich Park is a private pleasure ground occupying a bluff on the Thunderbolt river, a short distance east of Bonaventure, and commanding a magnificent view of the surrounding country. It is reached by a shell road branching from the Thunderbolt road at Bonaventure. A branch of the Coast Line railroad runs to the park entrance. The grounds are handsomely laid out. On the bank of the river is the dancing pavillion and back of it are the bowling alleys. The military rifle range is a short distance beyond. The park is the headquarters of the Savannah Rifle Association, and most of the military contests take place there. The place possesses some historic interest, from the fact that it was in the line of the city's defenses during the civil war, and in the attack of the French forces upon Savannah in 1779 Count Pulaski and a part of the French army encamped there on the march against the city.

TYBEE.

Tybee Island, the great seaside resort of the South, is at the mouth of the Savannah River. The greater part of the island is owned by the Tybee Beach Company. It is reached by a fifty minutes' ride over the Savannah and Atlantic railway. The route is for the greater distance in full view of the harbor and open to the free sweep of the ocean breezes. Twickenham, Bruton Hill, Deptford, Causton's Bluff and Mackey Point plantations present conspicuous attractions to the tourist. The magnificent stalwart oaks of Deptford, with their mammoth limbs, beautifully and gracefully draped with soft moss, constitute a grove equaling in grandeur the avenues of Bonaventure. Tybee beach, which has been pronounced superior to that of Cape May, extends a distance of five miles, and is a magnificent and solid roadway commanding a complete view of Tybee roads and the ocean. The surf bathing is unsurpassed. During the bathing season the beach presents a scene rivaling in a measure the panoramas of life and beauty which render Long Branch, Newport, Cape May and Nantucket renowned. It is lined with hotels, cottages and club houses from North End to the new Hotel Tybee at South End. The railroad runs within full view of the beach. The island is also accessible by steamers which land at North End.

Tybee is the most important link in the chain of islands which fringe the South Atlantic coast from Charleston to Fernandina. The most careful research has failed to fix definitely the exact time of its settlement, but from the best information it was occupied a short time previous to the settlement of Savannah by people from the neighboring South

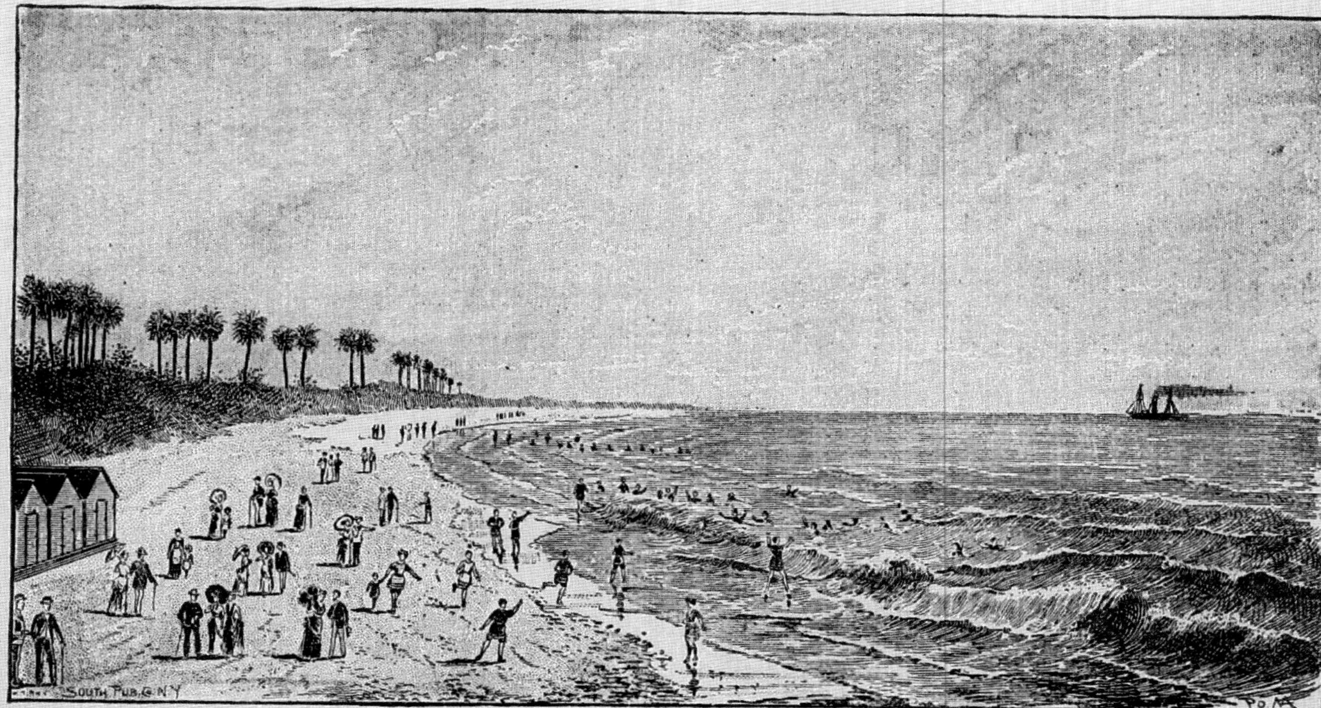

TYBEE BEACH.

Carolina islands. One of the most interesting and noteworthy incidents in connection with its history is that upon its soil John Wesley landed and uttered his first prayer in Georgia. As early as 1733 a lighthouse was built on the island by Oglethorpe, and a plate of the tower is in the Public Record office in London. The first fortification of any importance was built by the British. It was an earthwork, covered now by the site purchased by the United States government for a heavier defensive work, and was designed to guard the entrance to the Savannah River.

One of the most notable and conspicuous objects on the island, which is viewed with much interest by visitors, is the Martello Tower on the north beach in proximity to the lighthouse. It was built in the latter part of the last century by the United States government. It is a curious looking structure of a concrete of oyster shells and lime.

Among the historic memories which cluster around Tybee, is that of its being the scene of the first capture of a British vessel by an American commissioned man-of-war, in the struggle of the colonists. The first bombardment ever heard on the island was in September, 1779, when the English garrison at Fort Tybee was dislodged by the French. During the civil war the island was again fortified and occupied by a garrison, the Confederate troops taking possession April 13, 1861. It remained garrisoned until November 13th, when it was evacuated, the move being hastened by the capture of Port Royal by the Federal army, rendering the position of the garrison insecure and liable at any time to capture or isolation. Some time after the Confederate evacuation of Tybee, the island was occupied by the Federal forces and was made the base of their operations in forcing the surrender of Fort Pulaski. From its earliest history Tybee has been a conspicuous factor in the military annals of the State and Union, and its importance as the key to the defenses of the coast and river approaches has always been recognized. Its development as a seaside resort is the result of Savannah enterprise and capital. It has already

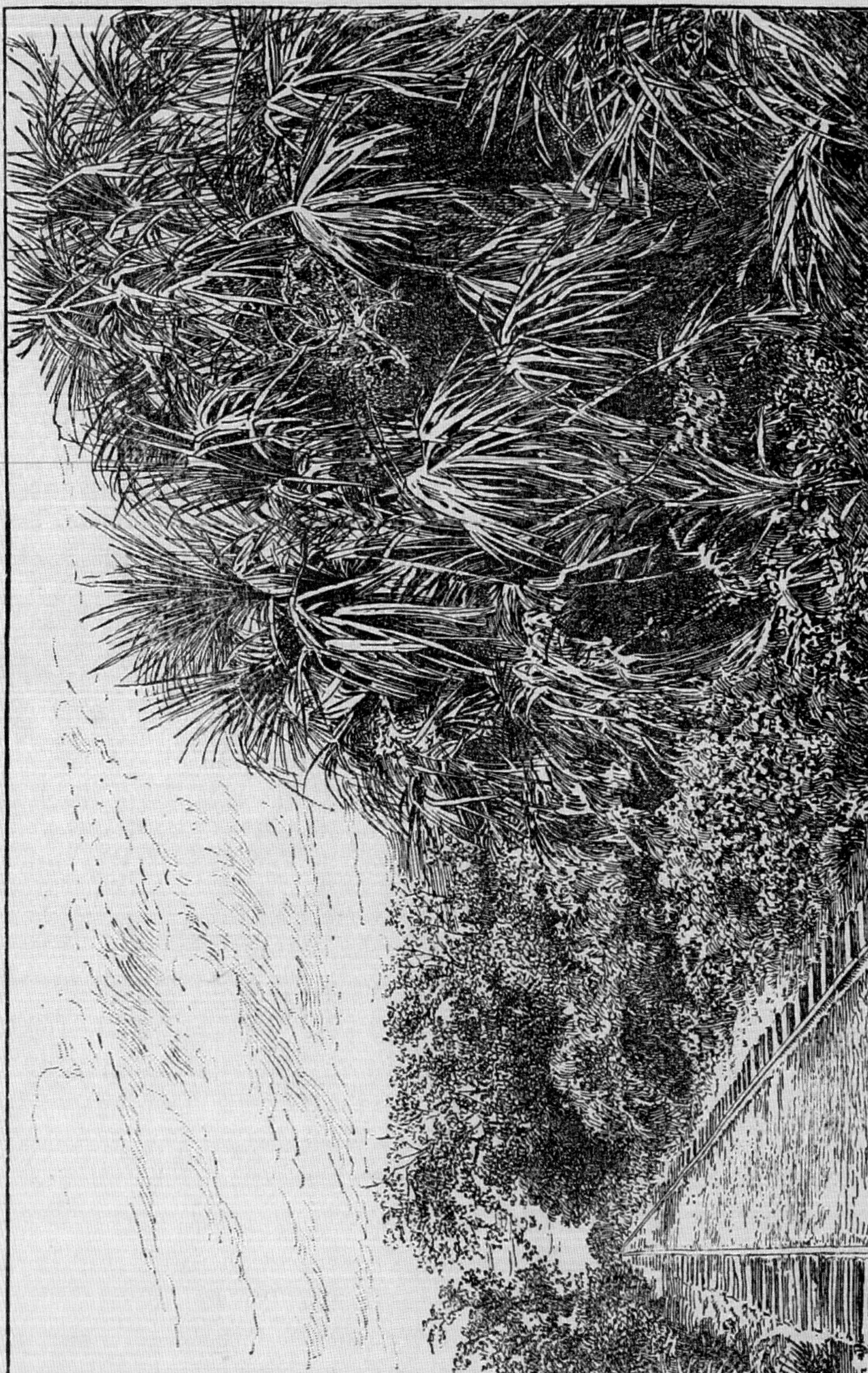

become the favorite resort of the South, and in 1889 the hotels were inadequate to the demands for accommodation, in the season's hight. The Savannah and Atlantic Railway was built in 1887 through the enterprise of D. G. Purse, Esq., the present president of the company, who has been, and is, largely interested in the development of the island. The Hotel Tybee is the finest seaside hotel on the South Atlantic coast.

ISLE OF HOPE.

Isle of Hope is the terminus of the main line of the City and Suburban railway, six miles from Savannah. It is charmingly situated on the banks of the Skidaway River. It was settled in 1737, four years after Savannah was founded. In the *London Journal* of 1744 an English tourist published an interesting account of his travels through Georgia, specially noting a visit to Isle of Hope and describing in vivid language the charming beauty of the place and the fortified residence of one of the early settlers, the ruins of which yet remain. The village is in the form of a horse shoe, and the visitor has from almost any point a sweeping view. From a straggling settlement it has grown to a pretty village, and is the summer home of many Savannahians. In an air line Isle of Hope is four miles from the ocean, and is directly opposite Skidaway Island. In the vicinity are numerous points of interest, among them the ruins of the fortified residence at "Wormsloe;" at the southern extremity of the island is a battery erected during the civil war and manned by the Confederate troops assigned for the protection of the coast. Not only as a place of visitation, but as a winter residence, Isle of Hope is one of the most charming and beautiful rural retreats on the coast.

MONTGOMERY.

Montgomery is the terminus of the Montgomery branch of the City and Suburban line, on the Vernon River, nine miles from Savannah. It was settled in 1801, and is one of Savannah's most picturesque suburban resorts. The ocean is in full view from the bluff overlooking the river, along which are beautiful avenues shaded by rows of magnificent oaks. Its healthfulness and the picturesqueness of its surroundings have made it a favorite spot. The waters in the vicinity abound, as they do at Isle of Hope, with fish, oysters, crabs and shrimp.

BEAULIEU.

Beaulieu is a charming resort on the Vernon River within view of Montgomery, and a few minutes' walk of the Montgomery terminus of the City and Suburban railway. It was settled in 1739 by William Stephens, the first president of Georgia. He gave it its present name on account of the fancied resemblance of the place to Beaulie, a manor of the Duke of Montgomery. By some the name was spelled Biewly. How it was changed to Beaulieu is not known. During Stephens' occupation of the place the settlers were constantly annoyed by predatory attacks by the Indians and Spaniards, and were compelled to fortify their homes in order to retain possession. During the Revolutionary war it was occupied by a small force of British troops. In September, 1779, a command of one thousand two hundred men, sent from the fleet of Count D'Estaing, in long boats, landed at Beaulieu and the British troops retired upon their approach. Several skirmishes between the opposing forces subsequently took place in the vicinity. The place is delightfully located, and is the site of a number of beautiful residences. It is about seven miles from the ocean.

WHITE BLUFF.

White Bluff, on the Vernon River, nine miles from Savannah, is the terminus of the White Bluff shell road, and is a popular place of resort. It is the summer home of a number of Savannahians. The village is on the bluff commanding a beautiful view of the river and the surrounding country. The fishing is excellent. The place is lacking in historical interest. A small Dutch settlement occupied the Bluff in 1740. The drive from the city is one of the most picturesque around Savannah. Two hours is ample for the drive and a rest at the village.

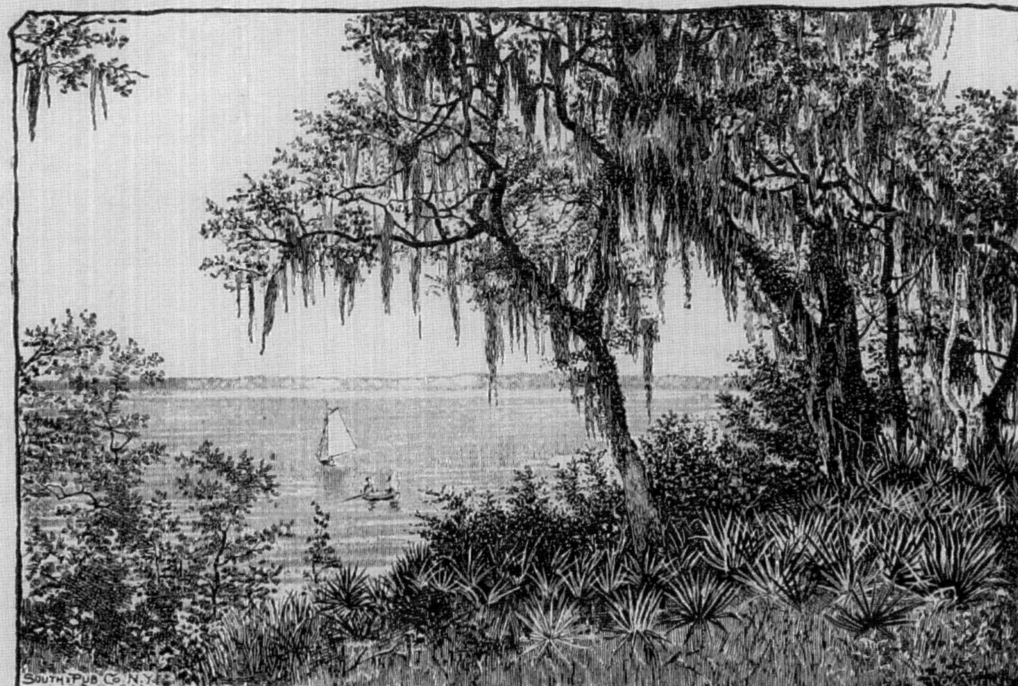

SCENE ON VERNON RIVER.

COMMERCIAL SAVANNAH.

SAVANNAH has always held a prominent place among the seaport cities of America on account of its commercial importance, because of its being the chief naval stores port of the world, and the second largest cotton port in America. It is the headquarters of five lines of ocean steamships, four lines of river steamers and of the two great railway systems of the South—the Central and Plant systems. The harbor, which extends eighteen miles from the city to the ocean, is filled with vessels from all parts of the world. The first steamship that ever crossed the Atlantic sailed from Savannah in 1819. The first cotton exported from Georgia was shipped from Savannah in 1788 by Thomas Miller, who afterwards became known under the sobriquet "Cotton Miller." In 1825, the first year in which there is any record of cotton exports, they were 64,000 bags. In 1889 they were over 800,000 bales. The cotton industry was of slow growth, however. Cotton growing had been experimented with for many years before Miller's venture, but it was many years later ere Savannah figured in the quotations as a cotton market. From 1821 Georgia took the lead in cotton production. The exports of cotton in 1872, amounting to 458,435 bales, of the value of $34,226,847, were increased in 1889 to 820,830 bales, of the value of $40,139,016. Receipts of cotton the present season will probably be one million bales. The exports of naval stores in 1880, the first year's business, amounting to 46,321 barrels spirits of turpentine and 231,242 barrels of rosin, of the value of $1,249,833, were increased in 1889 to 173,863 barrels of spirits and 610,302 barrels of rosin, of the value of $4,353,054. The total values of exports moved by water transportation alone have been increased from $34,266,847 in 1872 to $45,423,271 in 1889, and to a still larger figure in 1890. The value of importations in the same while has grown from $32,849,056 in 1872 to $55,062,710 in 1889. Among the exports from Savannah in 1753, according to the Historical Record, were 2,996 barrels of rice. At that early day, twenty years after the first settlement, rice was successfully cultivated. The rice exports from Savannah in 1889 were 45,000 barrels. The annual value of the exports of timber and lumber within the last fifteen years has risen from less than $500,000 to more than $1,400,000; that of fruits and vegetables from less than $500,000 to over $2,500,000; that of pig iron from about $25,000 to nearly $1,500,000; while that of cotton seed oil, a manufacturing industry not yet three years old at this port, reached last year a value of $850,000. The movement of commercial fertilizers by the great railway lines from Savannah will this year amount to 215,000 tons. Of this amount more than 50,000 tons have been manufactured in Savannah. The value of real estate and improvements has increased from a little over ten million dollars in 1865 to twenty million dollars in 1890, with corresponding increase in other values. The sections of country made tributary to Savannah by railway lines are among the richest in the United States in agricultural and mineral wealth, the latter as yet in the first stage of development, and its volume of increasing products will demand more extended facilities for movement.

For the establishment and support of a great trade center, the question of transportation is paramount to all other considerations. Savannah is well favored in this respect. It is the headquarters of two great railway systems, controlling over 3,500 miles of road—the Central railroad and the Plant systems.

Its steamship lines are the Ocean Steamship Company's and the New England and Savannah Steamship Company's lines between Savannah, Philadelphia, New York and Boston, and the Merchants' and Miners' Transportation Company's Savannah and Baltimore line. Other lines of transportation, less conspicuous, contribute to Savannah's commerce, but they are none the less important in their channels. The steamboats operating on the Savannah river between Augusta and Savannah, those engaged in the coasting trade south of Savannah, touching at Darien, and plying the St. Marys and St. Johns rivers, all, in a greater or less degree, add to the commerce of the port.

THE CLIMATE OF SAVANNAH.

The average annual temperature of Savannah is 66°; approximating the temperature of Bermuda, which is 68°; Gibraltar, Spain, 64°; Palermo, Sicily, 66°; Shanghai, China, 66°; Montevideo, South America, 66°; Cape Town, Africa, 66°, and Sydney, Australia, 65°. It is seldom that the temperature exceeds 85° in May, 90° in June, and 92° in August and September, although on rare occasions the mercury has gone higher, The highest temperature on record for Savannah is 105°, which occurred July 12, 1879. The lowest temperature known is 12°, which occurred January 12, 1886. The average date of killing frosts is November 28th. The weather is usually clear, the average number of cloudy days during the year being ninety. The summer comprehends more than one-half of the year; it begins in May and may be said not to end before November. A remarkable feature of the climate of Savannah is the cool nights, produced by the ocean breezes, which arise in the late afternoon. It is seldom that a hot night is experienced. The temperature is equable; from February to December it ranges from 70° to 92°, and this variation of 22° is seldom sudden, rather easy and gradual.

The following table of the highest, lowest, and average temperature, and the rainfall of Savannah, from 1870 to 1890, was compiled by L. A. Denson, observer U. S. Signal Corps, from the records of the Signal Bureau:

OBSERVATIONS COVERING NINETEEN YEARS.

	Jan.	Feb.	Mar.	Apr.	May.	Jun.	July.	Aug.	Sept.	Oct.	Nov.	Dec.
Average Temp.	51°	54°	59°	66°	74°	80°	81°	80°	76°	67°	58°	52°
Highest Temp.	80°	81°	87°	89°	98°	100°	105°	100°	96°	92°	83°	80°
Lowest Temp.	12°	19°	27°	33°	48°	50°	65°	63°	48°	37°	22°	15°
Rain (inches)	3.75	3.13	3.97	4.27	2.91	7.16	5.23	8.04	5.42	3.54	2.31	3.34

Season	Months	Average Temperature.	Rain (in inches.)
Winter	December, January, February	52°	10.22
Spring	March, April, May	66°	11.15
Summer	June, July, August	81°	20.43
Autumn	September, October, November	67°	11.27
Annual		66°	53.07

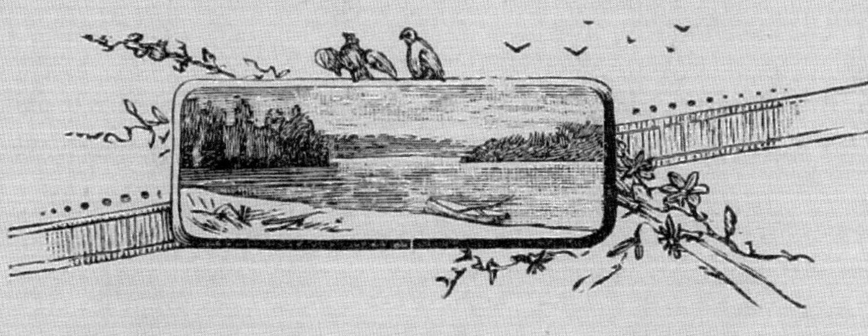

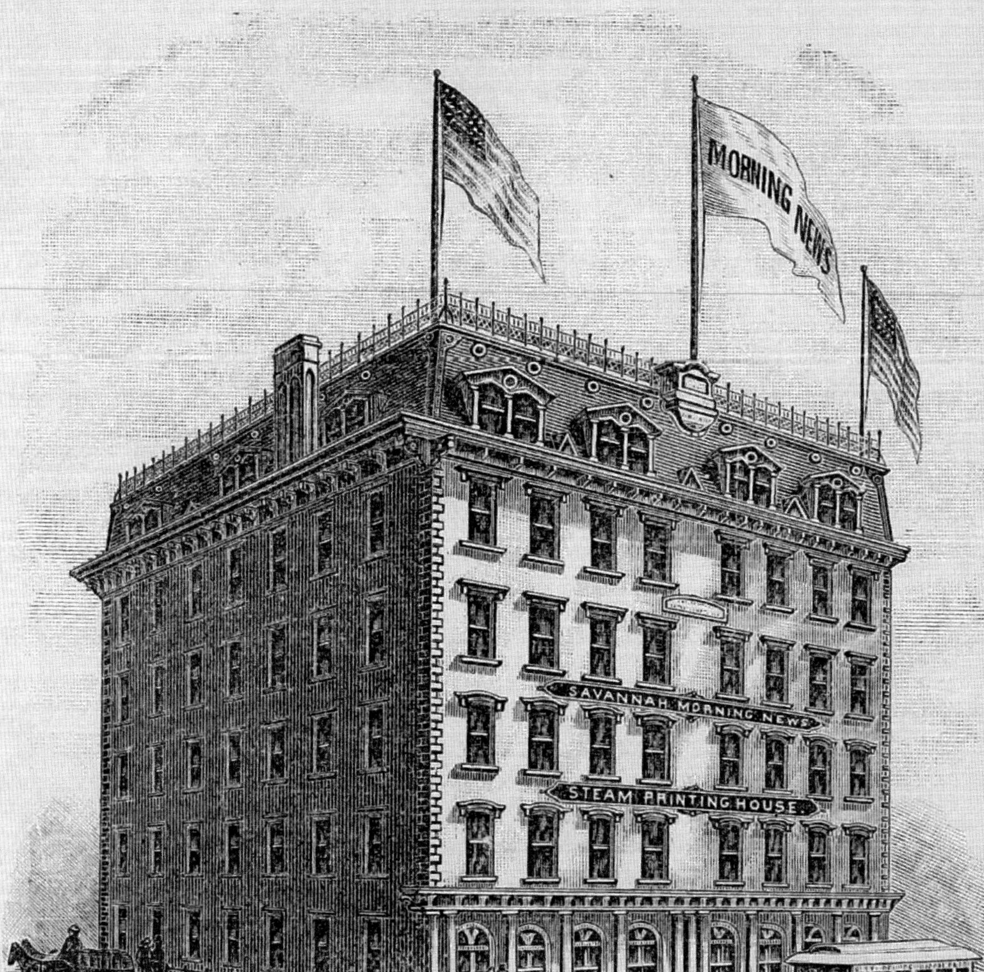
MORNING NEWS
SAVANNAH MORNING NEWS
STEAM PRINTING HOUSE

THE MORNING NEWS.

Savannah has had a newspaper since 1763. In April of that year the *Georgia Gazette* was established, and it lived through the days of the colonial government and those of the revolutionary period down to the closing years of the last century. From that time to the present there have been more than a score of newspapers published in this city. The most prominent of these defunct papers were the *Republican*, the *Georgian*, the *Courier*, the *Mirror*, the *Journal*, the *Evening Express*, and the *Advertiser*. The MORNING NEWS was a contemporary of all those mentioned, and is the only survivor of the newspapers of ante-bellum days. Leaving out those that died previous to 1861 we mention only those papers which are remembered by the present generation. The *Republican*, which was established in 1804, survived until 1874, when it was consolidated with a younger rival, the *Advertiser*, under the name of the *Advertiser Republican*. The new venture was not a success, and the rights and franchises of the concern were transferred to the MORNING NEWS, the consideration being the fulfillment of its contracts.

Savannah has always given a liberal support to its newspapers. Four morning papers and two afternoon papers have existed at one time, and there has never been a time within the past fifty years that the city has not had at least two daily papers—either two morning papers, or a morning and an afternoon paper.

THE MORNING NEWS made its appearance before the public in January, 1850. It was issued from No. 111 Bay street, where it had its quarters until it moved to where it is now published. It was a vigorous paper from the first, maintaining then, as it does to-day, the standard of honest Democracy, independent of the dictation of politicians. It passed through the great struggle of 1861–65, and came out, like all other Southern newspapers, in a rather dilapidated condition. In June, 1867, the present proprietor, Col. J. H. Estill, purchased an interest in the MORNING NEWS, and the following year he bought out the other owners, since which time he has retained the sole control.

Through the trying years, from 1865 to 1870, the MORNING NEWS maintained its position as a defender of the rights of the people, then threatened by carpet-baggers. It battled against those Radical leaders and their negro cohorts, who, with the aid of Federal bayonets, had seized the governments of the Southern States. It never compromised itself by in any way indorsing the rule of those plunderers or by recognizing their leaders. With the restoration of the government of the Southern States to the control of their people, Georgia became prosperous, and at once took her position as the Empire State of the South. In addition to its political course it was a newspaper without a rival as a news-gatherer. No other paper in the South had as yet awakened to the importance of furnishing live news. It organized the first system of special correspondents, and, for several years, was the only Southern paper that kept a regular correspondent at Washington and New York the year round. The MORNING NEWS has never turned aside from its line of duty as a newspaper to engage in personal controversies, but has never hesitated to defend the right or attack the wrong. It has always been its aim to furnish the latest news in the most acceptable form to its readers, and discuss all matters open to discussion in a fair and impartial manner. It has never believed that a newspaper was a place wherein any and every man should be permitted to vent his undigested and often prejudiced views on important public questions, but has asserted its right to be its own judge of what should go in its columns and what should not. In this progressive age there is probably no business that has undergone such great changes or has so much improved within the past twenty years as that of publishing a daily newspaper. A few years since a journal in the South that was provided with what is technically called a fast single-cylinder printing machine, of a capacity of 1,500 to 1,800 sheets per hour, was considered a well-equipped establishment. But few were provided with a machine for folding papers. In 1869 the MORNING NEWS introduced the first folding machine ever put to work in a daily paper office in Georgia, and it was considered by many a piece of reckless extravagance. Now the humblest of the dailies in the South folds its issues by machinery. About the same time the machine for putting the addresses of subscribers on papers was introduced into the MORNING NEWS office. This was the first mailer used in Georgia, if not in the entire South.

Fifteen years ago many morning papers "closed up" their forms by 10 to 12 o'clock in the evening, except on extra important occasions. One or two columns of telegraph news was considered a full service. With many it was supposed the zenith of newspaper publishing—at least in the smaller cities—had been attained. It was generally supposed that the limit of judicious expenditure had been reached. It had been with many newspapers. There was a remarkable decrease in the number of papers in the principal cities. The increased expenses could not be met by an augmented income, and the question was solved by the death of many old-time journals. The "fittest survived." The demand for later news caused the single-cylinder presses to give way to the double-cylinders. Provision was made against accidents, and duplicate presses, folding machines, engines and boilers added to the costly equipments. The telegraph service increased gradually from 1,800 words per day until it reached 6,000. These improvements were gradual. Five years ago, with one step almost, an immense advance was made on Southern journalism. This change was necessitated by the fast mails, which placed the large dailies of the North and West on the news-stands in many of the Southern cities some time during the day after their publication.

The newspapers had been improving, but the people's desire for news was still ahead of the supply. The first move to meet the new state of affairs was an increase in the service of the Associated Press. The quota of words per day was increased to almost double what it had been, and a better system of gathering news established and 4 o'clock in the morning became the closing hour. Here another difficulty presented itself—that of how to begin printing the edition of a morning paper at that hour and deliver it to all of its subscribers at the usual time. Everybody wants the latest news, and wants it at as early an hour as possible. A paper must not only be printed on time, but delivered on time, for the average reader of city papers would as soon go without his breakfast as without his favorite paper. The question of purchasing new and expensive machinery to overcome the time lost in waiting for the latest news was the next to present itself to the newspaper people. Some were in doubt as to the wisdom of investing a large sum of money in a perfecting press, which might scarcely be put in operation before a better one was invented. The price of the improved machines ranged from $30,000 to $50,000. The increasing circulations of the papers of the Northern and Western cities had long since developed the necessity for faster machines even than the immense eight and ten cylinder presses then used to print the metropolitan dailies, and as "necessity is the mother of invention," the perfecting press was evolved from the thoughts of many brains. The Web Perfecting Press developed new and presumably undreamed-of facilities. The smaller newspapers looked on amazed at the increasing demands upon their capital to meet the expense of perfecting presses. The price simply placed them beyond reach. The few newspaper men of this class who had enough money to buy one were more inclined to retire from business than to spend their all for a press. However, their hopes of a cheaper perfecting press, one suitable to the wants of the lesser dailies, were realized when ten years ago Hoe & Co. invented the perfecting press to print from movable type. This machine, costing about $30,000, was at once put into a number of offices. In 1884, however, the same firm invented a new machine, to print from stereotype plates, of much more simple mechanism. But three of these presses had been built when one was ordered from Messrs. Hoe & Co. for the MORNING NEWS. The introduction of the web perfecting press marked a new era in the newspaper business in Savannah.

The MORNING NEWS building is six stories high (with a well-lighted basement), and is surmounted by a two-story tower. The first floor is used exclusively for the business department. The space in front of the counter is paved with colored tiles. A neat iron railing encloses two-thirds of the floor, and inside is divided into the cashier's, the subscription clerk's and the advertising clerk's departments. In the rear is the proprietor's private office and another room for business purposes.

The MORNING NEWS consists of two distinct business establishments, under one name and one management, namely: The MORNING NEWS newspaper and the MORNING NEWS Steam Printing House. One-half of the building is almost exclusively used for the purpose of publishing and printing the DAILY AND WEEKLY MORNING NEWS, while the other half is entirely devoted to book and job printing, lithographing and blank book manufacturing.

The room next to the business office is the headquarters of the job departments. Speaking tubes connect this floor with each workroom, and an Otis passenger and freight elevator gives ready communication with the floors above and below. Speaking tubes also give ready means of communication between the counting room and the editorial, reportorial and newspaper composing rooms.

The second floor above the counting room contains the editorial and reportorial rooms. The composing rooms are on the sixth floor. The press rooms and stereotyping rooms are in the basement. The old-time pressman—not one so far back in the past as the days of the hand-press, but of later days—would not recognize as a familiar place the press-room of to-day. The immense printing machines, almost endowed with human intelligence, are inventions of late years. The forms of type as they come from the composing room in the sixth story are here stereotyped and the plates prepared for the press. After the plates are delivered to the pressman the press is ready to start in one minute. Two engines—one for driving the electric light dynamos, and the other for the perfecting press—occupy part of the adjoining room. The mail and delivery clerk has his headquarters in the basement. He is fenced out from the crowd of newsboys and newsmen who swarm about the office during the early hours of the morning, but is in such a position that no papers can go out without his knowledge. The departments other than those of the newspaper are well worthy of description. In no other establishment south of the Potomac river is to be found the same facilities for doing work as in the MORNING NEWS Printing House. It is as complete in all its details as it is possible for it to be without going beyond the bounds of what is legitimately connected with the "art preservative," and its kindred arts of lithography and book-binding. It would be an impossibility to minutely describe every little thing that contribute to make up the outfit of such an establishment. On the second floor is the lithographic press room. Lithography is a combination of chemistry and mechanics. It is a system of artistic printing in which the antagonism of oil and water are made to subserve a positive purpose in art. Lithography, or the art of producing impressions from stone, was accidentally discovered by Senefelder, a poor German musician and composer, who, because of his poverty, was unable to have his music engraved and printed. In his experiments to find a substitute for letter-press printing or copper or steel-plate engraving, he used a piece of oolitic limestone on which to distribute his ink. One day in copying a washing list for his mother, having no paper handy, he wrote on this stone what was required with the thick ink which he had ready for his experiments. He accidentally discovered that this writing gave forth an impression, and the idea occurred to him that by reducing that part of the surface of the stone on which there was no ink he might bring out the writing in relief, and thus print from it. He applied *aqua fortis* to the stone, and in a few minutes the uninked surface was reduced to the extent of the thickness of a sheet of paper. The art of lithography was thus established. Senefelder continued his experiments, and lived to see the art established, dying in 1834, the recipient of a pension from his King. The art of engraving on stone, transferring designs, and other methods now commonly in use, were discovered within the last third of a century. The steam presses now found in all complete lithographic establishments were even a more recent invention, only coming into general use about thirty years ago. This department of the MORNING NEWS does as good work as any place of the kind in the United States. The facilities are appreciated by the business men of the South, as is evidenced by the large amount of work bearing the office imprint to be found in every city and town. Among its best patrons are some of the largest cotton mills in Georgia and the Carolinas, while the tobacco men of Kentucky and Virginia, and the iron manufacturers of Georgia and Alabama contribute a liberal share of work.

On the fourth floor, north, is the job, book and press room. The place to see next is the book and job composing room. This adjoins the press room on the fourth floor, south. There are over 500 fonts of job type alone in this room, to say nothing of the hundreds of pounds of leads, rules, borders, etc., wood type, galleys, stones, and the hundred and one things that make up a complete printing office in which can be printed a visiting card or circus poster, or a ball programme or the Bible.

The bindery, which embraces the ruling, folding, forwarding and finishing departments, occupies the entire width and length of the fifth floor. It has a number of ruling, cutting, or trimming machines, and the steam embosser and the pagers. There are machines for perforating checks, and others for putting in eyelet holes, cutting out round labels (such as barrel labels printed in the lithographic room), pasteboard cutter, backing machines, dry presses, etc. Along the walls are shelves filled with leather and papers used in covering books, twines, threads, inks and other material for binders' use.

The next floor is the newspaper composing room, and above that the tower—a two-story mansard structure—the top being just a little over 110 feet from the pavement below. If the weather is clear, and it usually is, there is a magnificent view of the city and surrounding country. In the distance can be seen Tybee light, the Atlantic Ocean, &c.

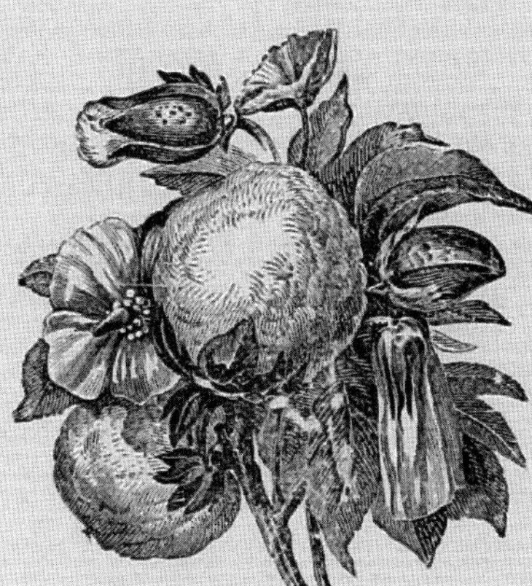

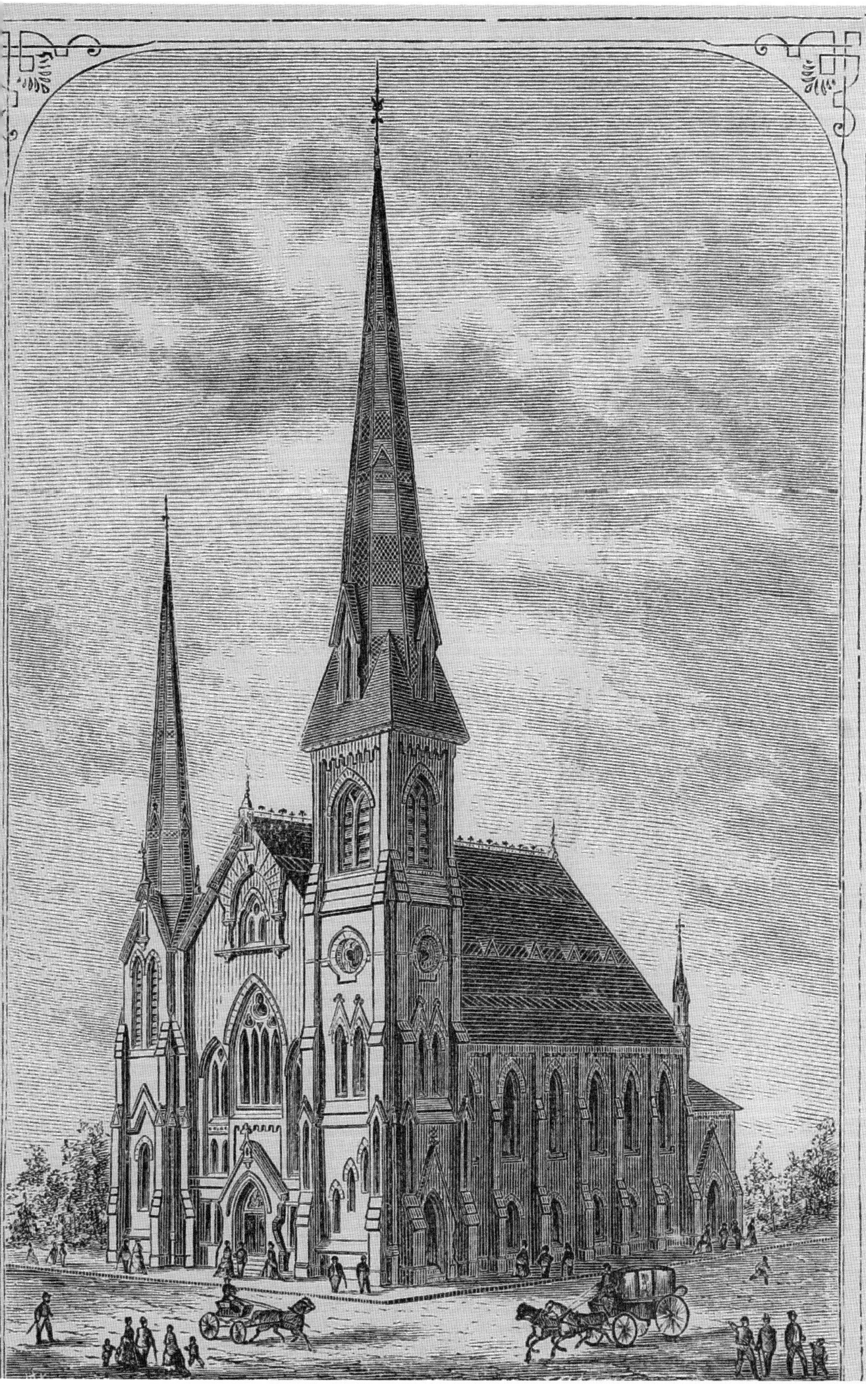

In and About Savannah.

HOTELS.

De Soto, corner Liberty and Bull, Madison Suare.

Pulaski, corner Bull and Bryan, Johnson Square

Screven, corner Bull and Congress, Johnson Square.

Marshall, Broughton between Abercorn and Drayton.

Harnett, corner Barnard and Bryan, Market Square,

POSTOFFICE.

Bay, corner Drayton. General Mail Delivery open 7 A. M. until 6 P. M. Money Order Office open 9 A. M. until 6 P. M.

TELEGRAPH COMPANIES.

Western Union, Main Office, Bull, corner Bay lane, opposite Custom House. Branch Offices:—Cotton Exchange Building and De Soto Hotel.

Postal Telegraph and Cable Company, main office Postoffice building, No. 99 Bay Street.

Southern Bell Telephone Co., Central Office, Sorrel Building, Bay and Bull.

DEPOTS.

Central Railroad of Georgia, West Broad and Liberty. Take Belt Line yellow cars, or any red car, and transfer to West Broad Street line.

Savannah, Florida and Western Railway and Charleston and Savannah Railroad (Atlantic Coast Line), Liberty and East Broad. Take Belt Line yellow cars, or any red car, and transfer to Liberty Street line.

City and Suburban Railway (Isle of Hope and Montgomery lines), Whitaker and Second. Take any red car and transfer to Abercorn and Whitaker Belt line.

Savannah and Atlantic Railway, President and Randolph. Belt Line yellow cars pass within a block, or take any red car and transfer to Liberty Street line. The City and Suburban Railway and the Belt Line have branch lines to the depot which are operated during the summer.

Coast Line Railroad (Bonaventure and Thunderbolt Dummy line), Bolton and East Broad. Belt Line yellow cars pass within a block, or take any red car and transfer to Habersham Street line.

WHARVES.

Ocean Steamship Company, Boston, New York and Philadelphia lines, foot of River Street. Take Belt Line yellow cars to foot of Indian Street, or omnibus from hotels.

Merchants' and Miners' Transportation Company, Baltimore line, foot of Bay Street. Take Belt Line yellow cars to Bay and East Broad.

Georgia and Florida Inland Steamboat Company, Florida line, foot of Lincoln.

Augusta Steamboat line foot of Drayton.

Savannah, Florida and Western Railway, naval stores and lumber wharves, foot of Bay. Take Belt Line yellow cars to Bay and East Broad.

STREET CAR LINES.

Abercorn and Whitaker Street Belt line, red cars, every ten minutes, round trip thirty minutes, passing City Exchange, Custom House, Postoffice, Cotton Exchange, Firemen's headquarters, old cemetery, Roman Catholic Cathedral, Savannah Hospital, Regimental Armory, through southern suburbs, around Forsyth Park and parade ground, with views of Confederate Soldiers' Monument, Georgia Historical Society Library, Masonic Temple and Morning News building, near all hotels, and connecting at Second and Whitaker Streets with suburban line to Isle of Hope and Montgomery. Fare five cents.

Liberty Street line, red cars, leave city market every ten minutes, through Barnard Street to Liberty, passing Odd Fellows' Hall, Telfair Academy of Arts and Sciences, Masonic Hall, De Soto Hotel, St. Vincent de Paul Convent, within a block of Cathedral, Charleston and Savannah and Savannah, Florida and Western Railway depots, to Tybee Railway depot. Fare five cents.

West Broad Street line, red cars, leave city market every ten minutes through Barnard Street to Liberty, passing Odd Fellows' Hall, Telfair Academy, Episcopal Orphans' Home and Central Railroad depot to Laurel Grove Cemetery. Fare five cents.

Belt line, circling the city, yellow cars, every ten minutes, round trip six miles, passing City Exchange, Custom House, Postoffice and Cotton Exchange, with view of the harbor from Bay Street, passing the Charleston and Savannah and Savannah, Florida and Western Railway depots and near Tybee Railway depot, through southern suburbs of city over high bridge, past Concordia Park and Kiesling's Gardens, and through 12th and Montgomery Streets, past Central Railroad depots and general offices, near all down town hotels, with transfer cars to the Ocean Steamship Company's wharves, Central and Gordon cotton presses and Planter's and Upper Rice mills, ice works and brewery. Fare five cents.

Coast Line, red cars, leave Broughton and West Broad Streets every ten minutes, passing the principal retail stores on Broughton Street, through Habersham Street, past police barracks, county jail and St. Joseph's Infirmary to Bolton Street junction, connecting with dummy line to Cathedral Cemetery, Bonaventure, Greenwich Park and Thunderbolt. Fare five cents to junction; junction to Thunderbolt and return twenty-five cents.

DRIVES.

To Thunderbolt over shell road, passing the Cathedral Cemetery, Bonaventure and Greenwich Park, with views of Thunderbolt River and the salt marshes, returning by direct road, four miles.

Out Bull Street, passing monuments and principal churches, around Forsyth Park and the military parade ground, passing Savannah Hospital, First Volunteer Regiment's Armory and Telfair Hospital on Drayton Street, over the White Bluff shell road, any distance, returning through Whitaker Street past the Georgia Historical Society Library to Bull Street.

To naval stores wharves below the city, along Bay Street past the Postoffice, Cotton Exchange, Custom House and City Exchange to the Ocean Steamship Company's wharves, passing cotton presses and warehouses, returning through River Street past the rice mills and through West Broad Street by Central Railroad depots and offices to Liberty Street—four miles.

SUBURBAN EXCURSIONS.

To Thunderbolt and Bonaventure, four miles, take Coast Line cars on Broughton or Habersham Streets to Bolton Street junction. Dummy trains make four trips daily to Thunderbolt. Fare round trip twenty-five cents.

To Isle of Hope six miles, Bethesda Orphan House eight and one-half miles, and Montgomery nine miles. Take Abercorn and Whitaker Street Belt line to Second Street depot. Suburban trains make trips daily. Fare round trip to Isle of Hope thirty cents; Bethesda and Montgomery fifty cents.

To Tybee Beach eighteen miles. Take Belt Line yellow cars or any red car and transfer to Liberty Street line to Tybee Railway depot foot of President Street. Two trains daily to the beach in winter and six in summer, passing naval stores and lumber wharves below the city, the overgrown earthworks of Fort Bartow one hundred acres in area, skirting rice fields and salt marshes with view of Thunderbolt River, along the banks of Savannah River south channel, passing at a distance Forts Oglethorpe and Pulaski, with a view of shipping at quarantine and in Tybee Roads, across Tybee Island and along the beach in full view of the ocean to South End. Fare round trip fifty cents.

THEATER.

Savannah Theater, Chippewa Square, Bull between Hull and McDonough. Box office, corner Bull and Congress.

ART GALLERY.

Telfair Academy of Arts and Sciences, Telfair Place, Barnard between State and President; open daily 10 A. M. until 5 P. M. Admission twenty-five cents.

LIBRARIES.

Georgia Historical Society, Whitaker and Gaston; open to members and non-residents. Library hours 10 A. M. to 9 P. M.

Catholic Library Association, Drayton, between McDonough and Perry. For members.

Young Men's Hebrew Association, (Masonic Temple), Liberty and Whitaker. For members.

Young Men's Christian Association reading rooms and gymnasium, Bull and Jones. Free reading room, open 8 A. M. until 10 P. M.

Savannah Port Society free reading rooms for sailors, Bay and Abercorn Street. Open daily 8 A. M. until 10 P. M.

POINTS OF VIEW.

City Exchange tower, Bay foot of Bull.
Morning New building, Bay and Whitaker.
Court House tower.
Solarium of De Soto Hotel.
Electric light towers. Permission from Superintendent of Brush Electric Light Works.

HALLS.

Masonic Hall, Liberty and Whitaker.
Catholic Library Hall, Drayton, between Perry and McDonough.
Odd Fellows' Hall, Telfair Place, Barnard and State.
Mozart Hall, St. Julian & Whitaker.
Armory Hall, Court House Square, Bull between State and President.
Metropolitan Hall, Whitaker and President.
Turner Hall, Broughton and Jefferson.
Yonge's Hall, Whitaker and Duffy.

MONUMENTS.

Confederate Soldiers, Parade Ground.
Pulaski, Monterey Square.
Jasper, Madison Square.
Gordon, Court House Square.
Greene, Johnson Square.
Gettysburg, Laurel Grove Cemetery.

BANKS.

Merchants' National, St. Julian and Drayton.

Southern Bank of the State of Georgia, Drayton between Bryan and St. Julian.

Savannah Bank and Trust Company, Bay and Drayton.

Central Railroad Bank, Bay between Bull and Drayton.

National Bank of Savannah and Oglethorpe Savings and Loan Company, Bryan Street, between Bull and Drayton.

Citizens' Bank, Drayton and Bryan.

C. H. Olmstead & Co's Banking House, Johnson Square between Bryan and St. Julian.

Title Guarantee and Loan Company,' savings department, Congress between Bull and Whitaker.

Germania Bank, Bryan and Abercorn.

Chatham Dime Savings Bank, Bull between Congress and Broughton.

PUBLIC BUILDINGS.

City Exchange, Bay foot of Bull.
Custom House, Bay and Bull.
Postoffice, Bay and Drayton.
Court House, Court House Square.
Cotton Exchange, Bay foot of Drayton.
Georgia Historical Society Library, Gaston and Whitaker.
Telfair Academy of Arts and Sciences, Telfair Place.
County Jail, Habersham, between South Broad and Liberty.
Police Barracks, South Broad and Habersham.
City Market, Market Square.

ARMORIES.

First Volunteer Regiment of Georgia, Abercorn and Huntingdon.

Chatham Artillery, Court House Square, Bull between State and President.

Savannah Volunteer Guards Battalion, Madison Square, Bull between Harris and Macon.

Georgia Hussars, Masonic Temple, Liberty and Whitaker.

NEWSPAPERS.

THE MORNING NEWS, daily, No. 3 Whitaker Street.
The Evening Times, daily, No. 98 Bryan Street.
Georgia Familien Journal, weekly, No. 89 Bay Street.
Savannah Independent, weekly, No. 5 Drayton Street.
Savannah Local, weekly, No. 1½ Bull Street.
Old Homestead, monthly, No. 42 and 41 Bull Street.

Savannah Tribune, (colored), weekly, No. 156 St. Julian Street.

CLUBS.

Oglethorpe Club, Bull and Broughton.
Catholic Library Association, Drayton between McDonough and Perry.
Young Men's Hebrew Association, Liberty and Whitaker.
Harmonie Club, Jones and Bull.
Savannah Volunteer Guards Battalion, Madison Square.
Travelers' Exchange, Bull and Congress.

SCHOOLS.

Chatham Academy, Bull and South Broad.
Barnard Street School, Chatham Square, Barnard and Taylor.
Massie School, Calhoun Square, Abercorn and Gordon.
Cathedral School, Perry and Abercorn.
St. Patrick's School, Liberty Square, Montgomery between President and York.
West Broad School, for colored children, West Broad foot of Congress.
East Broad Street School, for colored children, East Broad and Gaston.
St. Vincent de Paul Academy, Liberty between Abercorn and Lincoln.
Oglethorpe Seminary, Jones and Whitaker.
Richmond's Commercial Institute, Perry between Bull and Whitaker.
School for Boys, Macon between Bull and Drayton.
Savannah Academy, Madison Square, Bull between Macon and Charlton.
Haven's Industrial School, for colored girls, Anderson between Burroughs and Cemetery.

CONSULATES.

Argentine Republic—Rafael S. Salas, Vice Consul, 80 Bay.
Austria-Hungary — Edward Karow, Vice Consul, 108½ Bay.
Belgium — Leopold Charrier, Consul, 80 Bay.
Brazil—W. H. Adams, Vice Consul, 114 Bay.
British—Walter Robertson, Vice Consul, 89½ Bay.
Chili—R. B. Reppard, Consul, Gwinnett, on Savannah, Florida and Western Railway.
Denmark—C. M. Holst, Vice Consul, 120 Bay.
France — Frederick Chastanet, Vice Consul, 151 New Houston.
Germany—J. Rauers, Consul, 108½ Bay.
Italy—L. Trapani, Consular Agent, 112 Bay.
Netherlands—W. de Bruyn Kops, Consul, 76½ Bay.
Nicaragua—Rafael S. Salas, 80 Bay.
Peru—Rafael S. Salas, Consul, 80 Bay.
Portugal—A. V. Ivancich, Vice Consul, 94 Bay.
Russia—Joseph J. Wilder, Vice Consul, 112 Bay.
Spain—Narcisco Perez-Petinto, Consul, 120 Bay.
Sweden and Norway—C. M. Holst, Vice Consul, 120 Bay.
Uruguay—Rafael S. Salas, Consul, 80 Bay.
Venezuela—N. Frierson, Consul, 70 Bay.

HOSPITALS.

Savannah Hospital, Huntingdon between Drayton and Abercorn.
St. Joseph's Infirmary, Taylor and Habersham.
Telfair Hospital for Females, New Houston and Drayton.
Georgia Infimary for colored people, Sixth between Abercorn and Lincoln.

ASYLUMS.

Female Orphan Asylum, Madison Square, Bull and Charlton.
Episcopal Orphan's Home, Liberty and Jefferson.
Home of the Friendless, Charlton and Drayton.
Abram's Home, Broughton and East Broad.
Bethesda Orphanage, Bethesda, eight and one-half miles from city.
Widow's Home, President and West Broad.
Little Minnie Mission, Jones and Lincoln.
St. Mary's Orphan Home, Habersham and St. Paul.
Little Sisters of the Poor, Drayton and Perry.
Sacred Heart Orphanage, for colored children, Habersham and St. James.

CEMETERIES.

Bonaventure, Thunderbolt shell road. Take Coast Line cars and Dummy line, or drive over Thunderbolt shell road.

Laurel Grove, Anderson Street. Take Barnard and West Broad Street red cars.

Cathedral Cemetery, Thunderbolt shell road. Take Coast Line cars and Dummy line.

Old Cemetery, South Broad and Abercorn. Permission to visit from police headquarters.

DISTANCES FROM SAVANNAH.

NORTH AND WEST.

	Miles.		*Miles.*
Boston	1146	Toledo	970
New York	917	Detroit	1035
Philadelphia	826	Chicago	1028
Baltimore	730	St. Paul	1557
Washington	688	Cincinnati	768
Pittsburg	990	St. Louis	904
Buffalo	1195	Kansas City	1232
Cleveland	1012	Denver	1871

SOUTH.

	Miles.		*Miles.*
Memphis	745	Atlanta	294
Nashville	586	Macon	191
Chattanooga	434	Columbus	291
Knoxville	558	Montgomery	385
Richmond	572	Birmingham	448
Wilmington	327	Mobile	464
Charleston	115	New Orleans	666
Asheville	360	Thomasville	200
Aiken	140	Brunswick	100
Augusta	132	Waycross	96

FLORIDA.

	Miles.		*Miles.*
Jacksonville	172	Sanford	296
St. Augustine	208	Altamonte	309
Tallahassee	301	Winter Park	314
Pensacola	420	Orlando	318
Monticello	224	Suwanee Springs	172
Fernandina	205	Kissimmee	336
Magnolia	200	Bartow	381
Green Cove Springs	201	Silver Springs	276
Palatka	228	Ocala	278
De Land	282	Homasassa	335
Enterprise	294	Gainesville	249
Rock Ledge	344	Tampa	411
Titusville	331	Punta Gorda	457

HISTORICAL SUMMARY OF SAVANNAH.

1733—Oglethorpe landed with the colonists February 1.
The town laid off and the first house begun October 9.

1734—Arrival of the Salzburgers March 12.

1736—John and Charles Wesley arrived February.

1737—George Whitefield arrived May.

1738—Tomo-Chi-Chi died.

1740—The first Christ church begun.
Bethesda Orphan House founded March 25.

1743—Oglethorpe left the colony finally July 11.

1744—The first commercial house established by James Habersham and Charles Harris.

1751—The first colonial assembly met January 15.

1752—Georgia became a royal province.

1754—Governor Reynolds, the first governor, arrived October 29.

1758—The Church of England established by law.

1759—The first wharf built.

1763—The first printing press established and the "Georgia Gazette," the first newspaper, published April 7.

1764—Robert Bolton, the first postmaster appointed.

1775—First meeting of Provincial Congress January 18.

1776—First attack by the British on Savannah March 3.
Capture of the first British vessel in the Revolutionary war by an American schooner, off Tybee, July 10.

1777—The State Constitution formed and Christ Church Parish named Chatham County after the Earl of Chatham.

1778—The city captured by the British December 29.

1779—Battle of Spring Hill and death of Count Pulaski and Sergeant Jasper October 9.

1783—The city evacuated by the British forces July 11.

1784—The first legislature assembled January.

1786—The Chatham Artillery organized May 1.
General Nathaniel Greene died June 19.

1788—The first cotton exported from Savannah.
The Chatham Academy incorporated.

1789—The city incorporated.

1790—John Houston elected the first Mayor.

1791—Washington visited Savannah, May 12.

1796—The first destructive fire occurred November. Two hundred and twenty-nine houses burned.

1799—The City Exchange built.

1802—Vice-President Aaron Burr visited Savannah May 20.

1804—Great storm; over 100 negroes drowned on Hutchinson's Island, September 8.

1810—First census taken, Savannah's population 5,195.

1814—Capture of British brig-of-war "Epervier" by American sloop-of-war "Peacock" May.

1819—President James Monroe visited Savannah and participated in the dedication of the Independent Presbyterian church May.
The first steamship to cross the Atlantic sailed from Savannah May 20.

1820—The second great fire, destroying 460 houses, January 11.

1825—Lafayette visited Savannah March 18.

1854—President Fillmore visited Savannah April 22.

1861—Occupation of Fort Pulaski by Confederate forces January 3.
Confederate State convention met in Savannah and ordinance of secession framed March 7.

1862—Bombardment and capture of Fort Pulaski, by Federal forces, April 10.

1864—The city invested by Sherman's army, after the march to the sea, December 13.
Fort McAllister captured December 11.
Evacuation of Savannah by the Confederate army December 20.
The city formally surrendered December 21.

1879—Corner stone of Jasper monument laid October 9.

1881—Great storm and tidal wave August 28.

1883—The Sesqui Centennial of the city celebrated February 14.
Third great fire occurred October 31, 365 houses in Yamacraw burned.

1886—The Chatham Artillery's centennial celebrated May 1.
Savannah shaken by earthquake August 31.

1888—President Cleveland visited Savannah and the Jasper monument unveiled February 22.

1889—Fourth great fire April 6.

1890—Corner stone of Independent Presbyterian church relaid Jan. 13.

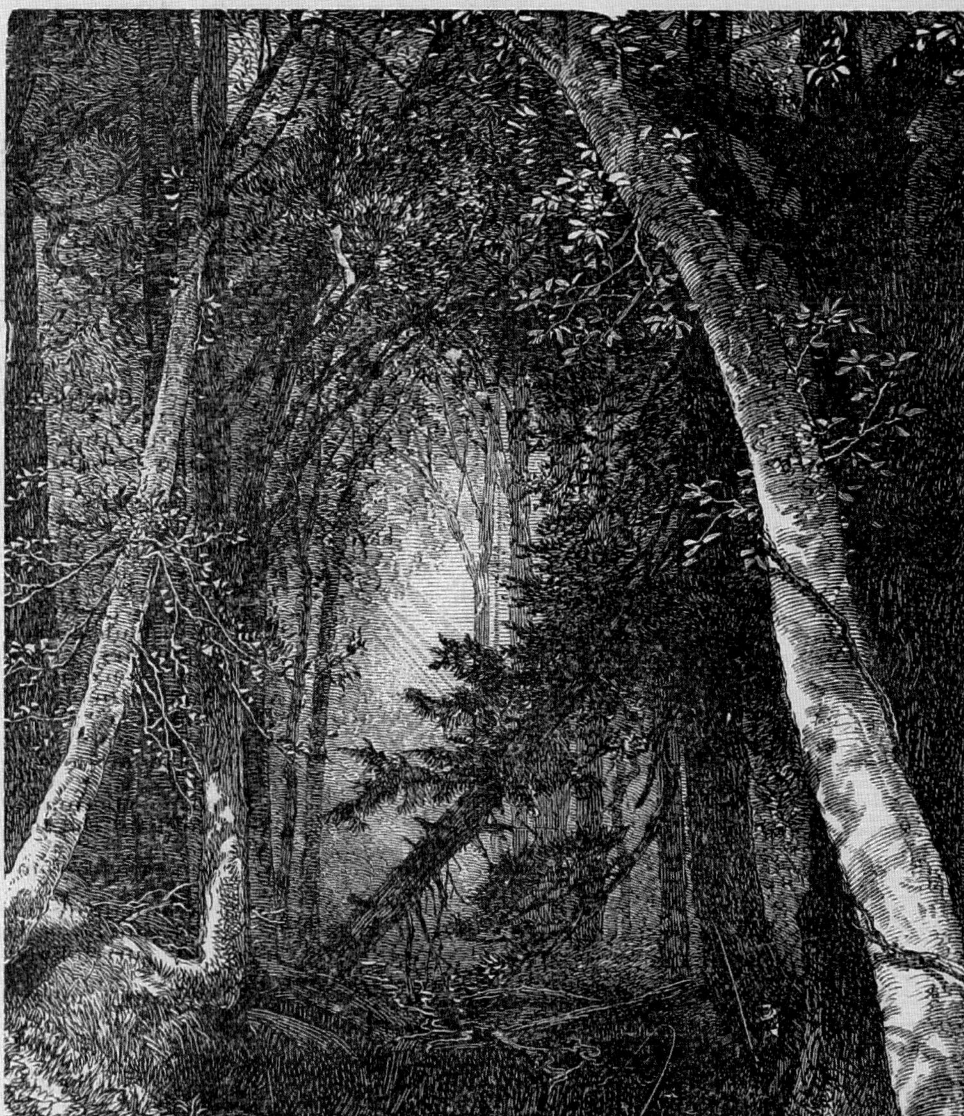

JOHN FLANNERY, *President.* **JAMES SULLIVAN,** *Cashier*
HORACE A. CRANE, *Vice-President.*

SOUTHERN BANK

OF THE STATE OF GEORGIA.

Drayton Street, between Bryan & St. Julian Streets,

SAVANNAH, GA.

Capital, $500,000. Surplus, $500,000.

DEPOSITORY OF THE STATE OF GEORGIA.

SEMI-ANNUAL STATEMENT

At Close of Business December 31st, 1889.

Loans and Discounts	$2,220,410 63
Bonds and Stocks	692,065 00
Banking House and other Real Estate	72,603 26
Furniture and Safes	2,000 00
Due by Banks and Bankers	68,378 29
Protest Account	4 75
Cash	348,675 10
	$3,404,137 03

Capital Stock	$500,000 00	
Surplus Fund	500,000 00	
Undivided Profits	127,930 98—	$1,127,930 98
Dividend No. 37 unpaid	90 00	
Dividend No. 38, payable Jan. 1st, 1890	30,000 00—	30,090 00
Due Depositors		1,953,633 58
Certified Checks		13,292 48
Due Banks and Bankers		222,792 29
Due Treasurer State of Georgia		56,397 70
		$3,404,137 03

DIRECTORS:

EUGENE KELLY, of Eugene Kelly & Co., New York.
JOHN FLANNERY, of John Flannery & Co., Savannah, Ga.
S. B. PALMER, of Palmer Brothers, Savannah, Ga.
E. A. WEIL, of Meinhard Bros. & Co., Savannah, Ga.
HORACE A. CRANE, Savannah Ga.
J. B. DUCKWORTH, of Duckworth, Turner & Co., Savannah, Ga.
LEE ROY MYERS, of Lee Roy Myers & Co., Savannah, Ga.
HORACE P. SMART, Pres. Amoskeag Lumber Co., Savannah, Ga.

Rowland & Myers,

REAL ESTATE AGENTS,

94 BAY STREET,

SAVANNAH, - - - - - GEORGIA.

Property Bought and Sold Strictly on Commission.

CALL AND SEE US BEFORE INVESTING.

R. M. DEMERE,

—DEALER IN—

Stocks, Bonds

AND

Real Estate.

No. 5 Drayton Street,

"Real Estate is the Basis of All Wealth."

THOSE WHO HAVE OPERATED IN

REAL ESTATE

IN SAVANNAH AND CHATHAM COUNTY THROUGH

C. H. DORSETT,

Real Estate Dealer,

142 Congress Street

HAVE REALIZED THE TRUTH OF THE ABOVE AXIOM.

ALWAYS TO BE HAD THROUGH HIM:

Residence and Business Property,
Farms, Suburban Lands for Sub-Division,
Manufacturing Sites, Etc.

Correspondence is solicited with Home or Foreign syndicates desiring to purchase local industries.

THE SAVANNAH LINE.

OCEAN STEAMSHIP COMPANY OF SAVANNAH,

AND

NEW ENGLAND AND SAVANNAH STEAMSHIP COMPANY.

For NEW YORK, BOSTON, PHILADELPHIA,

AND ALL

EASTERN POINTS.

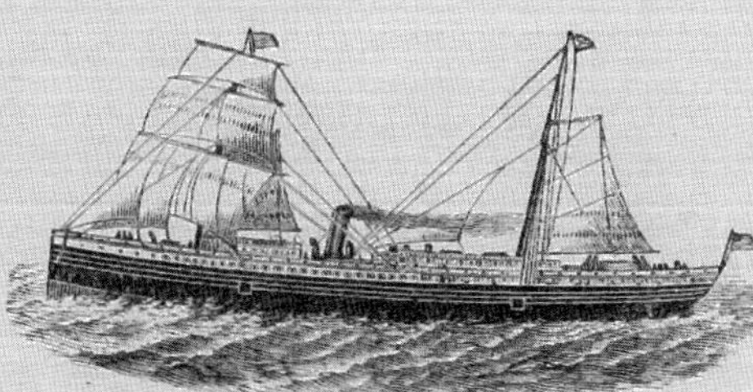

THE FLEET.

Kansas City	4,000 tons	City of Birmingham	3,000 tons
City of Augusta	3,000 tons	City of Savannah	2,100 tons
Tallahassee	3,000 tons	City of Macon	2,100 tons
Chattahoochee	3,000 tons	Gate City	2,100 tons
Nacoochee	3,000 tons	Dessoug	1,500 tons

LEAVE SAVANNAH

FOR NEW YORK

Mondays, Wednesdays, Fridays and Saturdays.

Passengers for Philadelphia connect with Bound Brook Route.

For BOSTON,. - - - - - - - EVERY FOUR DAYS.

For PHILADELPHIA, (For Freight Only.) EVERY TEN DAYS.

G. M. SORREL, General Manager. SAVANNAH, GA.

C. G. ANDERSON, Agent. SAVANNAH, GA.

Merchants' and Miners'

TRANSPORTATION CO.

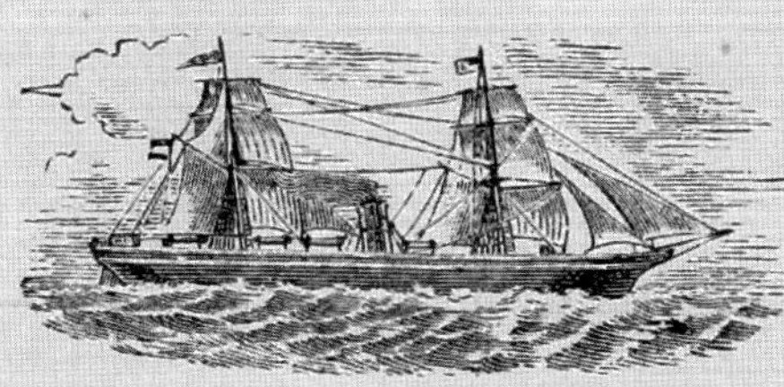

The Steamships of this Company Ply Regularly Between

Savannah and Baltimore,

Baltimore and Boston AND

Baltimore and Providence.

Close connections at Savannah with the CENTRAL RAILROAD, the S., F. & W. R'y, and the different Steamboat Lines.

Leaving Savannah for Baltimore every Five Days, and from Baltimore for Savannah on Same Days.

The Baltimore Route is the most direct between the South and West. It is also the most economical and quickest.

The Steamers are first-class in every respect, with excellent accommodations for passengers. Reduced rates of passage to emigrants from Baltimore and all points West and Southwest.

This Company's Steamers are especially arranged for the transportation of fruit and vegetables, the Savannah, Florida and Western Railway tracks running on Steamer's wharves, and Through Bills of Lading at low rates will be issued.

A. L. HUGGINS, Agent,
Baltimore, Md.

W. E. GUERARD, Agent,
56 Bay Street, Savannah.

The South Florida Railroad.

"GATE CITY" ROUTE.

ACROSS THE STATE FROM

ST. JOHN'S RIVER TO THE GULF OF MEXICO.

Double Daily Trains Between **Jacksonville and Tampa.**

Through Line, carrying U. S. Mail between New York and West Indies.

PULLMAN PARLOR CARS, PULLMAN BUFFET CARS,
NEW YORK TO PORT TAMPA,

PASSING THROUGH THE

Richest Orange Belt of Florida.

SCENERY UNSURPASSED.

At PORT TAMPA, the deep water terminus of this line, connection is made with the elegant steamers of the

PLANT STEAMSHIP LINE

— FOR —

KEY WEST AND HAVANA.

The trains run direct to the ship's side at Port Tampa. For full information, time cards, etc., address

WILBUR McCOY, G. T. A., Sanford, Fla.

COAST LINE RAILROAD.

THE ONLY RAIL LINE TO

BONAVENTURE,

THUNDERBOLT.

GREENWICH PARK

AND FOR **WARSAW BEACH.**

TWENTY ‡ MINUTES ‡ RIDE ‡ FROM ‡ THE ‡ CITY.

A delightful trip through charming scenery, passing the CATHEDRAL CEMETERY and the OLD FORTIFICATIONS.

FOUR TRAINS DAILY.

COMFORTABLE CARS. -:- STEEL RAIL TRACK.

☞Take Habersham Street cars to COAST LINE DEPOT twenty minutes before departure of suburban trains, or take Liberty Street cars in front of the De Soto and transfer at Habersham Street.

Special Cars for Charter for Excursions.

CITY AND SUBURBAN RAILWAY.

—THREE TRAINS DAILY TO—

Isle of Hope, ✻ Montgomery,
Beaulieu, Bethesda.

THIRTY MINUTES RIDE

Over smooth track along a charming route to Savannah's Famous

Resorts on the Salts AND Historic Bethesda.

THE PULASKI

SAVANNAH, GA.

Watson & Powers, Proprietors.

* * * * * * * * *

THE FAVORITE STOPPING PLACE FOR TOURISTS.

* * * * * * * * *

OPEN ALL THE YEAR.

Accommodations for 250 Guests.

The PULASKI is in the center of th business portion of the city, fronting Bull Street, the favorite promenade, and Johnson Square. An entire Southern Exposure. The most delightful location in the city.

The hotel has been remodeled and enlarged; another story has been built; fifty rooms have been added; the dining room doubled in size, and reception and reading rooms added with new and elegant furnishin,s.

Electric Lights, Otis Hydraulic Elevator, and Artesian Water, Hot and Cold Baths.

—:— *The Cuisine and Service Unsurpassed in the South.* —:—

Every Convenience and Luxury for * * * * * * * * * * **the Comfort and Enjoyment of Guests.**

All lines of horse cars within one minute's walk of the Hotel. Omnibus at all Trains and Steamers. Rooms secured by telegraph. ADDRESS

WATSON & POWERS,

SAVANNAH, GA.

THE OCEAN ROUTE.

Savannah & Atlantic R'y.

TYBEE ISLAND

—WITH ITS—

Grand Beach,
Magnificent Surf Bathing,
and Pure Air.

THE GREAT SUMMER AND WINTER SEASIDE RESORT OF THE SOUTH ATLANTIC.

FIFTY MINUTES' RIDE FROM SAVANNAH

Over a Smooth Road FREE from Dust and Cinders, Swept by Ocean Breezes Nearly its Entire Length.

5 REGULAR TRAINS DAILY 5

COMFORTABLE COACHES,
COURTEOUS CONDUCTORS,
AND PERFECT ORDER
MAINTAINED ON ALL TRAINS.

An Excursion Route at all times safe for Unattended Ladies and Children.

Excursion, (ROUND TRIP,) 50 Cents.

FAMILY EXCURSIONS—Tuesdays and Fridays.

Family Excursion Days, fare, round trip, ADULTS.................................35 CENTS
CHILDREN, 5 to 12 years...20 CENTS

The only through line running to the Ocean without connecting steamboats, terminating at the Finest Beach on the Atlantic Coast for surf bathing, and for seven miles affording a magnificent drive.

FINE HOTELS. SPACIOUS PAVILIONS.
ARTESIAN WELLS.

The road newly equipped with fast trains.
All street car lines lead to the depot in the city.

H. H. WOODRUFF,
General Agent.

D. G. PURSE,
President and Manager.

The De Soto

SAVANNAH, GA.

Opened January 1st, 1890.

JOHN A. BAKER & CO., Proprietors.

330 ROOMS

THE DE SOTO was built in 1889, and is the most luxuriously appointed Hotel in the South. It is in the center of the city, occupying an entire square, fronting the principal promenades and drives, and is near all public buildings and libraries and points of interest. It is richly furnished, lighted with electricity, heated throughout with steam and open fire places; is provided with hydraulic elevators, artesian water baths, and every appointment which tends to the perfect enjoyment of its guests.

ITS CUISINE AND SERVICE UNSURPASSED.

A MAGNIFICENT TOURISTS' HOTEL

With Every Luxury Obtainable.

Address

JOHN A. BAKER & CO.

THE PULASKI HOUSE

LIVERY AND TRANSFER STABLES,

138 and 140 Bryan Street.

ADJOINING THE PULASKI HOUSE.

All orders for Liveries and Transfers Promptly Filled.

Finest Double and Single Teams in the City.

OMNIBUS LINES BETWEEN ALL HOTELS, DEPOTS AND STEAMSHIP WHARVES.

Elegant Turnouts for drives to Thunderbolt, Bonaventure, White Bluff, and all Suburban Resorts.

TRANSFER AND BAGGAGE EXPRESS WAGONS AT EVERY TRAIN AND STEAMER.

Telephone Orders promptly responded to at all hours.

TELEPHONE No. 12.

Tourist Patronage a Specialty.

E. C. GLEASON,

PROPRIETOR.

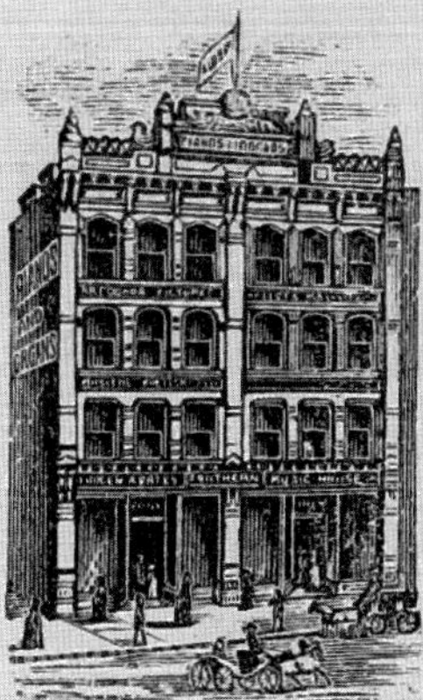

Savannah, Ga.

✠ Ludden & Bates ✠

SOUTHERN MUSIC HOUSE.

For 20 Years the Leading Southern Dealers.
in

PIANOS AND ORGANS

ALWAYS REPRESENTING THE

→ BEST MAKERS ONLY. ←

Each Name a Guarantee of Excellence.

Chickering Pianos.
The Legitimate Standard of the World. Over 77,500 in use.

Mason & Hamlin Pianos.
"The Greatest Improvements in Pianos in Half a Century."

Mathushek Pianos.
Silver-Toned. The Piano for a Lifetime.

Sterling Pianos.
High Grade Instruments at a Low Grade Price.

Mason & Hamlin Organs.
Leaders Always. Victors at all World's Contests. Best and Cheapest.

Sterling Organs.
Best Medium Price Organ Produced. Beautiful Styles at Small Cost.

NOTICE

Our One Price System.
Fifteen Days Test Trial.
All Freight Paid.
Complete Outfit Free.
Six Years Guarantee.

NOTICE

Our Exchange Privilege.
Best Instruments Made.
Lowest Prices Known.
Easy Installment Plans.
Fair Business Methods.

CORRESPONDENCE INVITED. CATALOGUES FREE.

LUDDEN & BATES SOUTHERN MUSIC HOUSE,

Savannah, Georgia.

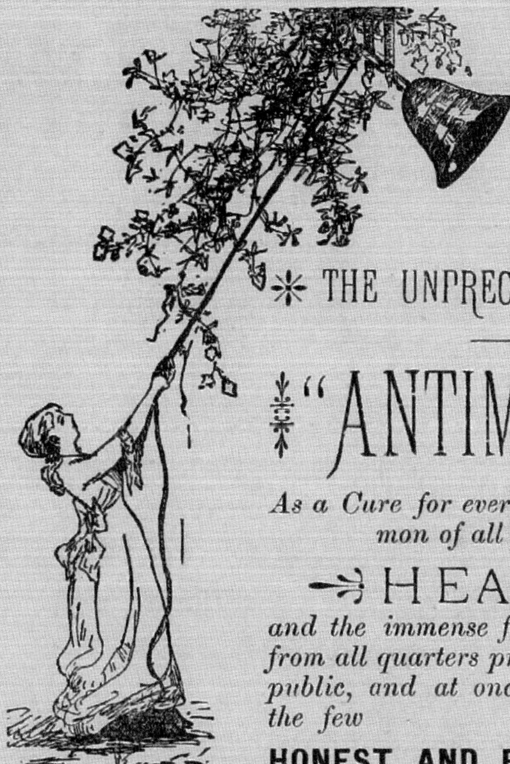

AN ENVIABLE

RECORD

BASED ON

True ✠ Merit.

✳ THE UNPRECEDENTED SUCCESS ✳

—— OF ——

"ANTIMIGRAINE"

As a Cure for every variety of that most common of all physical ailments,

HEADACHE.

and the immense favor which has greeted it from all quarters proves its acceptability to the public, and at once establishes it as one of the few

HONEST AND RELIABLE REMEDIES.

"Antimigraine" Contains no **Antipyrine, Morphine, Chloral, Cocaine,** or other poisonous drugs or chemicals, and can be taken freely without fear of serious or unpleasant after effects. It is not a Cathartic, does not disarrange the stomach. It is Perfectly Safe and in action it is always Sure and Speedy.

MACON, GA., August 12, 1889.
The Antimigraine Company.

GENTLEMEN:—I have been using "Antimigraine" for nervous sick headache, and have given it to several of my friends who join me in stating that "Antimigraine is the best medicine for headaches we have ever taken and the only one which gives us quick and permanent relief without leaving unpleasant after effects.

Yours very truly,
MRS. W. F. ADAMS.

SAVANNAH, GA., June 3, 1889.
The Antimigraine Company.

GENTLEMEN:—It affords me no little pleasure to add my testimonial to the indorsement of your Headache cure "Antimigraine," for it has never failed to give me instant relief, with no unpleasant after effects that are generally brought about by so-called headache remedies.

Very truly yours,
REV. JAMES L. GILMORE,
Chaplain to Seamen.

ANTIMIGRAINE Is a beautiful wine colored liquid, pleasant to the taste, put up in bottles containing Twelve Full Doses. Sells for 50 Cents by all Druggists, and is Guaranteed to Cure all Headaches.

GARDNER'S

30½ Bull Street.

FLORISTS' AGENT

AND **HEADQUARTERS** FOR

CURIOSITIES.

Orange Walking Canes,
Live and Stuffed Alligators,
Alligator and Boars' Teeth Jewelry,
Shells, Ornamental Grasses.

FLOWER and GRASS SEEDS, BULBS, PLANTS,

Camelia and Palms in Every Variety.

FLOWER POTS AND PLANT FOOD.

AGENT FOR **OELSCHIG'S NURSERY**

Cut Flowers, Floral Designs and Baskets of All Descriptions Beautifully Made Up.

Camelia Flowers Packed and Shipped in Season a Specialty.

BIRDS, CAGES, MOCKING BIRD FOOD, BIRD SEEDS, MEDICINES AND TONIC.

J. GARDNER, Agent.

THE NEW YORK of the SOUTH.

SAVANNAH the largest and most prosperous city on the South Atlantic Coast; has more railroads than any other Coast city, and in two years will double its present number. It has the best deep water facilities of any Southern city, and is the largest naval stores depot in the world.

—SAVANNAH'S POPULATION 60,000.—

THE CITY'S PRESENT GROWTH AND PROGRESS POINT TO 200,000 POPULATION IN 1900.

Property that sold two years ago for $50 an acre is now selling for $500 per acre and in two years will sell for $5,000 per acre more.

Harmon, Walker & McHarrie,

SAVANNAH'S LEADING

REAL ESTATE FIRM

No. 156 Broughton Street,

Buys, sells and handles Real Estate strictly on commission. As we are not speculating we are in a position to advise our customers on this subject. We will not sell or handle property held at an unreasonable price. If you wish a home, a farm, business property, mineral or timber lands we can supply you. None can yet say they made a mistake by purchasing through us.

BUSINESS TRANSACTED FOR NON-RESIDENTS.

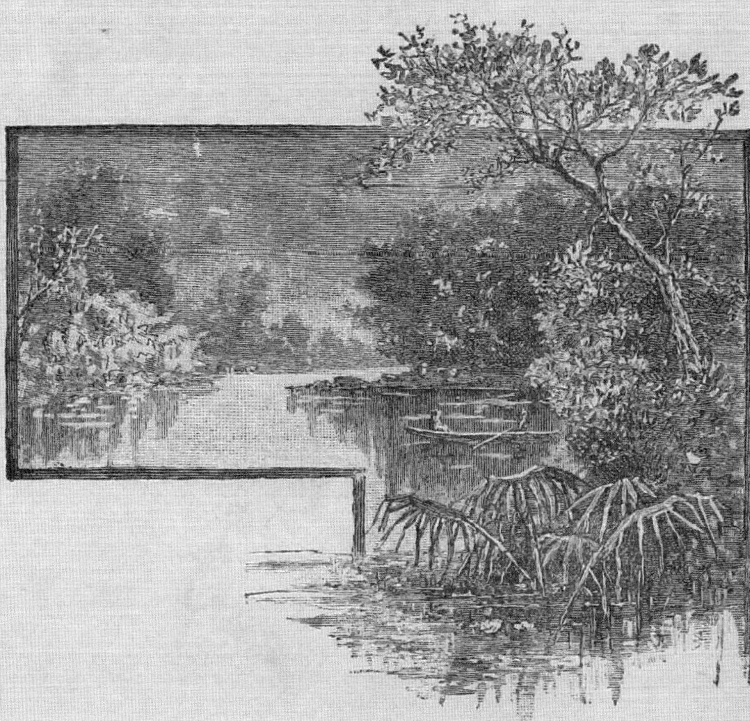